Cooks in a Hurry
Cooking for Friends

by
Fiona
Williams

foulsham
LONDON • NEW YORK • TORONTO • SYDNEY

foulsham

The Publishing House, Bennetts Close,
Cippenham, Slough, Berks SL1 5AP, England.

ISBN: 0–572–02309–x

Typeset in Garamond and Trump Mediäval by
Ann Buchan (Typesetters), Shepperton, Middlesex
Printed in Great Britain by
St Edmundsbury Press, Bury St Edmunds, Suffolk

Contents

Thanks and Acknowledgements

Many of the recipes in this collection have been given to me by family, friends and colleagues. I would like to thank my husband, Tom; my brother, Tim; my friends, Nicky, François, Marga, Nick and Liz; my neighbour, Annika; La Plagne chalet host, Theo, and hostesses, Louise, Keri, Debbie and Katie; Tignes chalet hostess, Louise; and Ski Beat guests, Evs and Jembo.

Notes on Recipes

• Ingredients are given in metric, imperial and American measures. Use only one set per recipe, do not interchange.

• All spoon measures are level.

• Eggs are size 3 unless otherwise stated.

• Always wash fresh produce and peel where necessary before preparing according to the recipe.

• All herbs are fresh unless dried are specified. If substituting dried when fresh are called for, use only half the quantity (or less) as dried are very pungent.

• All preparation and cooking times are approximate.

• Always cook in the centre of the oven unless otherwise stated and pre-heat the oven (if necessary) to the temperature specified in the recipe.

Introduction

*I*nviting friends to supper is so much more enjoyable if you can sit down with them feeling and looking relaxed. This is impossible if you've been slaving over a complicated meal for hours, even more so if you've already had a tiring day. Easy entertaining and good food is more about confidence and planning than following fiendishly difficult, slavishly trendy and hideously expensive recipes. The important things are to balance your menu for colour, flavour, texture and cost; select good food carefully; cook it simply; and finally, serve it with a flourish (even if you are a bit nervous).

The recipes in this collection are the ones I have found to be really successful for entertaining. Many of them were tried and tested in the French Alps where I cater for winter and summer chalet parties. In these chalet parties the number of guests varies from three to sixteen and it is necessary therefore to use recipes which are easy to adapt to greater or smaller quantities and of course are quick and simple to prepare. When catering for chalet parties, there are budgets to be adhered to, so it goes without saying that these recipes are economical too.

Easy Entertaining

*H*aving guests for a meal can be a daunting prospect. But with a little careful planning – and this book – it will be as easy as winking! The key is to keep everything simple. Choose a well balanced menu (there is a whole range of samples to choose from in this chapter). Prepare and cook ahead as much as possible, so you only have the last-minute finishing touches to do when your guests have arrived.

Setting the Scene

*O*nce the table is laid, I always feel I'm nearly organised. The bare essentials are:

- A clean cloth and/or table mats.

- Preferably enough cutlery and crockery for all the courses, (so you don't have to wash up rapidly in between). Lay it starting with the first course cutlery on the outside, working in towards the mats. Knives and spoons go on the right, forks on the left. Dessert cutlery can be on the inside or at the top of the mats, spoons facing left, forks underneath, facing right.

- Paper or linen table napkins (unless you're good at origami, either fold attractively on the side plates or fold in half diagonally to form triangles, fold in the two base corners and place in the wine glasses).

- If you're serving different drinks with each course, it is customary to have different glasses. But for more informal affairs, one is enough (and it means less washing up!). The glasses should be at the top right of each place setting.

- As a centrepiece, have fresh flowers or a small candlestick with a candle. Don't make it too large or your guests won't be able to see over it and there won't be enough room for all the food!

- Keep the lighting subtle, but not too dark so they can't see what they're eating.

- Have background music playing quietly even before they arrive. It helps break the ice and adds atmosphere.

- Make sure the rooms are warm but not too hot. Your guests will get very warm during dinner with all the good food and wine!

- Don't offer too many nibbles – it will dull their appetites. However, a few nuts or crisps is a good idea – especially for the drinkers – you don't want them sozzled before they eat.

The Drinks

*O*nce you've chosen your menu, you'll need to decide what you are going to serve to drink.

Wines

It's usually accepted that you serve a dry white with starters, fish or white meat; a red wine with game, red meat or cheese; a sweet white with desserts; and rosé with anything you like! Many people don't serve wine with soup (although a glass of sherry would go down well) and there isn't much point in serving wine with highly spiced foods – chilled lager is best. But having said all the above, I believe you should serve whatever you enjoy most with anything you like.

• Allow ½ bottle per person.

• Always offer mineral water and/or a non-alcoholic alternative too; there is a large choice of non-alcoholic wines, or sparkling apple or grape juice.

Before Dinner

You can either offer a whole selection – spirits and mixers, sherry, lager etc. – or just a cocktail. Kir (blackcurrant liqueur and white wine) or Buck's Fizz (sparkling wine and orange juice) are both popular and available ready mixed. Alternatively, just offer a choice of wine or beer/lager – plus soft drinks of course.

• Don't have too many cook's nips to calm your nerves – you need a clear head to dish up!

After Dinner

Some people like to offer port, brandy or liqueurs with coffee. Others stick to more wine for the hardened drinkers. For many of us, a cup of good coffee and an after dinner mint chocolate are the perfect end.

Sample Menus

Lardon Salad
Spiced Beef Casserole
Galettes, Fried Peas and Garlic
Brandy Snap Baskets

Moreish Onion Soup
Chicken with Piquant Caper Relish
Carrots with Orange and Cardamom
Broccoli and Potato Bake
Frozen Coffee Crunch Soufflés

Tomato and Carrot Soup
Italian Lamb
Orange Glazed Turnips, Artichoke and Potato Bake
Valentine Apples

Grilled Goat's Cheese Salad
Redcurrant Beef
Creamed Spinach, Tagliatelle
Meringue Peaches

Velvet Leek and Potato Soup
Thai Grilled Fish
Zingy Carrots and Courgettes, Buttered New Potatoes
Mandarin and Chocolate Cheesecake

Light Tomato Soup
A Plate of Smoked Salmon with Side Salad
Swedish Potatoes, Brown Bread and Butter
Chocolate and Pear Pie

Spanish Prawns
Peppered Duck Breasts
Re-fried Beans, Antibes Potatoes, Buttered Carrots
Scarlet Salad

Watercress Soup
Leek and Goat's Cheese Pie
Baked Fennel and Tomatoes, Green Salad
Tiramisu

Piquant Mushrooms on Garlic Toasts
Carpaccio con Salsa Verde
Pasta with Vegetable Ribbons, Soy Garlic Beans
Whisky Oranges and Atholl Brose Cream

Cajun Wings
Marinated Salmon Steaks
Potatoes and Anchovy Cream, Broccoli
Brandy Chocolate Roulade

Tuna and Sweetcorn Bisque
Leg of Lamb in Red Wine
Creamy Courgette Bake, Buttered Carrots, Roast Potatoes
Almond Pear Flan

Fried Goat's Cheese
Chicken with Tarragon Cream
Baked Sliced Potatoes, Sweetcorn
Garlicky Green Beans
Kiwi Pavlova

Prawns in Garlic Butter
Turkey Escalopes in Ginger Wine
Mustard Roast Potatoes, Peas, Cauliflower and Almonds
Chocolate Mousse

Courgette, Tomato and Basil Soup
Pescada à la Marina
Lemon Potatoes, Salad
Apple and Orange Brûlée

Guacamole and Salad Sticks
Mushroom and Cashew Nut Pilaff
Tomato Salad
Banoffee Pie

Smoked Trout Salad
Carbonnades à la Flamande
Baked Potatoes, Green Beans, Turkish Fried Carrots
Crème Caramel

Pepper Provençale
Melting Moments Chicken Cordon Bleu
Classic Potatoes with Cream, Sweetcorn, Broccoli
Lemon Curd Mousse

Mushrooms in Cumin and Coriander Sauce
Trout in Lemon Butter Sauce
New Potatoes, Stir-fried Vegetables
Tom's Chocolate Gateau

Prawn Provençale
Peppered Steak
Baked Sliced Potatoes, Mixed Salad
Orange with Yoghurt Sauce

Smoked Mackerel Pâté
Pork Tenderloin and Mushrooms
Rice, Green Salad
Crêpes and Chocolate Cream

Starters

*Y*our chosen starter should set the scene for the whole dinner party. It should whet the appetite for what is to follow – not dull it completely. Balance is all-important. There are loads of sample menus (see page 9), but as a general rule avoid similar ingredients, or similar cooking methods in both starter and main course. For instance, you wouldn't serve Piquant Mushrooms on Garlic Toasts followed by Creamy Mushroom Steaks or a soup followed by a casserole. Mix and match, varying flavours, textures and colours throughout the meal.

Moreish Onion Soup

*I*n this recipe, the onions are caramelised to a sweet, rich brown with a delectable flavour. If you fry slices of French Bread in garlic butter then top with grated cheese (preferably Gruyère (Swiss)), and place them in the bowls of soup, it makes an excellent light lunch.

SERVES 6	METRIC	IMPERIAL	AMERICAN
Onions, thinly sliced	1 kg	2¼ lb	2¼ lb
Olive oil	45 ml	3 tbsp	3 tbsp
Beef stock, hot	900 ml	1½ pts	3¾ cups

TO GARNISH
Croûtons

1   Fry (sauté) the onions gently in the oil for 15 minutes, covered, until soft.

2   Remove the lid and increase the heat, letting the onions caramelise to a rich brown, stirring regularly to dissolve the deposits on the base of the pan. Continue like this for 30 minutes; it may seem excessive, but the more caramelised the onions are, the better the flavour will be.

3   Pour in the stock, bring to the boil, then simmer for about 20 minutes.

4   Garnish with croûtons or the cheesy toasts as described in the introduction.

PREPARATION TIME: 10 MINUTES
COOKING TIME: 65 MINUTES

Velvet Leek and Potato Soup

This soup has a delicious flavour and a wonderful smooth texture but needs a garnish, such as snipped chives or finely grated orange rind scattered over cream or yoghurt.

SERVES 4	METRIC	IMPERIAL	AMERICAN
Leeks, sliced	3	3	3
Unsalted (sweet) butter	25 g	1 oz	2 tbsp
Potatoes, diced	225 g	8 oz	2 cups
Chicken OR vegetable stock	600 ml	1 pt	2½ cups
Single (light) cream	75 ml	5 tbsp	5 tbsp
Salt and pepper			

TO GARNISH
A little double (heavy) cream OR plain yoghurt
Snipped chives OR grated orange rind

1   Fry (sauté) the leeks in the butter for 5 minutes.

2   Add the potatoes, stock and seasoning, bring to the boil, cover and simmer for 20 minutes.

3   Leave to cool slightly, then liquidise in a blender or food processor until smooth. Stir in the cream and re-season if necessary.

4   Reheat and serve ladled into warm soup bowls and garnish each with a swirl of cream or yoghurt and a sprinkling of chives or grated orange rind.

PREPARATION TIME: 10 MINUTES
COOKING TIME: 30 MINUTES

Watercress Soup

*T*urn this into an exciting lunch dish by placing a lightly poached egg in each bowl of soup instead of the hard-boiled egg garnish.

SERVES 6	METRIC	IMPERIAL	AMERICAN
Onion, finely chopped	1	1	1
Olive oil	30 ml	2 tbsp	2 tbsp
Watercress	350 g	12 oz	¾ lb
Plain (all-purpose) flour	15 ml	1 tbsp	1 tbsp
Chicken stock	1 litre	1¾ pts	4¼ cups
Salt and pepper			
Double (heavy) cream	60 ml	4 tbsp	4 tbsp

TO GARNISH
2 hard-boiled (hard-cooked) eggs, finely chopped

1   Fry (sauté) the onion in the oil in a saucepan for 2 minutes until soft.

2   Roughly chop the watercress, reserving a few small sprigs for garnish. Add the chopped watercress to the onion and cook for 2 minutes. Stir in the flour.

3   Gradually stir in the stock and seasoning and simmer for 30 minutes. Purée the soup in a processor so that it is smooth but still speckled.

4   Add the cream and reheat gently. Serve garnished with the chopped egg and tiny watercress sprigs.

PREPARATION TIME: 5 MINUTES
COOKING TIME: 35 MINUTES

Spiced Carrot Soup

*T*his wonderful, orange-flavoured soup can be served hot but is also delicious served chilled.

SERVES 4	METRIC	IMPERIAL	AMERICAN
Finely grated rind of orange	1	1	1
Onion, finely chopped	1	1	1
Carrots, chopped	450 g	1 lb	1 lb
Piece root ginger, peeled and crushed	5 mm	¼ in	¼ in
Piece cinnamon stick	5 cm	2 in	2 in
Chicken stock	750 ml	1¼ pts	3 cups
Fresh orange juice	200 ml	7 fl oz	scant 1 cup
Salt and pepper			
Plain yoghurt	60 ml	4 tbsp	4 tbsp
Egg yolk	1	1	1

TO GARNISH
Orange rind, cut into matchsticks

1   Place all the ingredients, except the yoghurt and egg yolk, in a saucepan. Bring to the boil and simmer for 25 minutes.

2   Cool the soup slightly, remove the cinnamon stick and liquidise in a blender or food processor until smooth. Return to the rinsed-out pan.

3   Beat the yoghurt and egg yolk, add a little of the soup and stir, then return all this mixture to the pan. Heat through gently, but do not boil.

4   Serve hot, garnished with orange rind.

PREPARATION TIME: 10 MINUTES
COOKING TIME: 30 MINUTES

Light Tomato Soup

This tomato soup is nothing like the cream of tomato soup available in tins. This is fresh tasting with a Mediterranean flavour.

SERVES 4	METRIC	IMPERIAL	AMERICAN
Onion, finely chopped	1	1	1
Olive oil	30 ml	2 tbsp	2 tbsp
Passata (sieved tomatoes)	500 ml	17 fl oz	2¼ cups
Juice and coarsely grated rind of 1 orange			
Juice of ½ lemon			
Water	250 ml	8 fl oz	1 cup
Salt and pepper			
A pinch of sugar			

1 Fry (sauté) the onion in the oil until soft but not brown.

2 Add the passata, orange juice, lemon juice and water.

3 Simmer for 20 minutes.

4 Season to taste with a little salt, pepper and the sugar and serve garnished with the grated orange rind.

PREPARATION TIME: 5 MINUTES	
COOKING TIME: 25 MINUTES	

Provençal Fish Chowder

SERVES 7–8	METRIC	IMPERIAL	AMERICAN
Olive oil	60 ml	4 tbsp	4 tbsp
Small onion, finely chopped	1	1	1
Leek, trimmed and finely sliced	1	1	1
Garlic cloves, crushed	2	2	2
Ripe tomatoes, skinned and diced (or canned)	350 g	12 oz	¾ lb
Bouquet garni	1	1	1
Bay leaf	1	1	1
Potatoes, diced	225 g	8 oz	½ lb
Fish stock	1.5 litres	2½ pts	6 cups
Tomato purée (paste)	15 ml	1 tbsp	1 tbsp
White fish, skinned, boned and cubed	750 g	1½ lb	1½ lb
Dried basil	15 ml	1 tbsp	1 tbsp
Small black olives, stoned (pitted) and halved	50 g	2 oz	⅓ cup
Salt and pepper			

1   In a large pan heat the oil and cook the onion, leek and garlic gently for 5 minutes, until soft. Add the tomatoes and cook for about 10 minutes.

2   Add the herbs, potatoes, stock and tomato purée. Cover and simmer for 15 minutes until the potatoes are cooked.

3   Add the fish to the soup with the basil and olives. Cook until the fish is just tender, season and remove the herbs. Serve at once.

PREPARATION TIME: 15 MINUTES

COOKING TIME: 35 MINUTES

Carrot and Coriander Soup

*C*arrots and coriander compliment each other perfectly and the sweetness is enhanced by the addition of a few sultanas.

SERVES 4	METRIC	IMPERIAL	AMERICAN
Small onion, finely chopped	1	1	1
Garlic clove, crushed	1	1	1
Carrots, finely chopped	450 g	1 lb	4 cups
Olive oil	30 ml	2 tbsp	2 tbsp
Coriander (cilantro) seeds, crushed	5 ml	1 tsp	1 tsp
Ground coriander	5 ml	1 tsp	1 tsp
Vegetable stock	900 ml	1½ pts	3¾ cups
Sultanas (golden raisins), chopped	50 g	2 oz	⅓ cup
Salt and pepper			
Double (heavy) cream	20 ml	4 tsp	4 tsp
Chopped coriander	15 ml	1 tbsp	1 tbsp

1   Fry (sauté) the onion, garlic and carrots in the oil in a large pan for 10 minutes.

2   Stir in the crushed and ground coriander and cook for 1 minute.

3   Add the stock. Cover and simmer for 15 minutes until the carrots are tender.

4   Let the soup cool slightly. Liquidise in a blender or food processor, return to the pan, add the chopped sultanas, salt and pepper and reheat gently.

5   Ladle into warm soup bowls and garnish with a swirl of cream and the chopped coriander.

PREPARATION TIME: 10 MINUTES

COOKING TIME: 28 MINUTES

Tuna and Sweetcorn Bisque

*H*ere is another easy soup that can be made in advance of dinner and reheated when needed. A lovely variation (as I discovered when short of tuna) is to add prawns and reduce the tuna quantity.

SERVES 4	METRIC	IMPERIAL	AMERICAN
Small onion, finely chopped	1	1	1
Butter	25 g	1 oz	2 tbsp
Mild curry powder	5 ml	1 tsp	1 tsp
Turmeric	5 ml	1 tsp	1 tsp
Paprika	5 ml	1 tsp	1 tsp
Plain (all-purpose) flour	25 g	1 oz	¼ cup
Chicken stock	450 ml	¾ pt	2 cups
Milk	450 ml	¾ pt	2 cups
Grated rind of ½ lemon			
Can sweetcorn (corn), drained	350 g	12 oz	1 large
Can tuna, drained	185 g	6½ oz	1 small

TO GARNISH
Chopped parsley

1   Cook the onion in the butter until soft. Stir in the curry powder, turmeric, paprika and flour. Cook for 1 minute, stirring all the time.

2   Gradually stir in the stock and bring to the boil, stirring constantly. Add the milk, lemon rind and sweetcorn. Simmer for a further 5 minutes.

3   Stir in the tuna. Simmer for a further 5 minutes. Serve sprinkled with parsley to garnish.

PREPARATION TIME: 5 MINUTES
COOKING TIME: 15 MINUTES

Courgette, Tomato and Basil Soup

*T*his is a very quick and easy soup to make (cheap too), yet it tastes really rich and is very filling. The flavours develop if you prepare it in advance then reheat when ready to serve.

SERVES 4	METRIC	IMPERIAL	AMERICAN
Butter	25 g	1 oz	2 tbsp
Onion, finely chopped	1	1	1
Courgettes (zucchini), coarsely grated	350 g	12 oz	3 cups
Garlic clove, crushed	1	1	1
Vegetable stock	600 ml	1 pt	2½ cups
Can chopped tomatoes	400 g	14 oz	1 large
Tomato purée (paste)	15 ml	1 tbsp	1 tbsp
Chopped basil leaves	30 ml	2 tbsp	2 tbsp
Salt and pepper			
TO GARNISH			
Double (heavy) cream	60 ml	4 tbsp	4 tbsp
Basil leaves			

1   Melt the butter in a large pan. Add the onion and cook until soft. Add the courgettes and garlic and cook for 3–4 minutes.

2   Add the stock, tomatoes and their juice and the tomato purée. Bring to the boil. Cover and simmer for 15 minutes. Add the chopped basil and season to taste.

3   Ladle into warm soup bowls and serve garnished with a swirl of cream and a few basil leaves.

PREPARATION TIME: 5 MINUTES

COOKING TIME: 25 MINUTES

Prawns in Garlic Butter

I usually allow 6 prawns (shrimp) per person, but the quantities are variable according to appetite. This is a great fun starter as no cutlery is needed – but remember the finger bowls and extra paper napkins.

SERVES 4	METRIC	IMPERIAL	AMERICAN
Unsalted (sweet) butter	100 g	4 oz	½ cup
Large prawns (jumbo shrimp) in their shells	24	24	24
Garlic clove, crushed	2	2	2
Chopped parsley	30 ml	2 tbsp	2 tbsp
TO SERVE			
Crusty French bread			

1   Melt the butter in a large shallow frying pan (skillet). Add the prawns and garlic at the same time.

2   Gently heat the prawns through and sprinkle on the parsley. Serve with fresh French bread to mop up the buttery sauce.

PREPARATION TIME: 2 MINUTES
COOKING TIME: 3 MINUTES

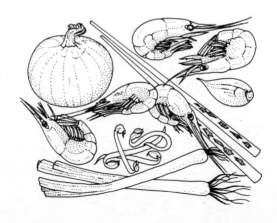

Piri Piri Prawns

This is an unusual spicy starter, not for the faint-hearted! Have plenty of drinks on hand, just in case.

SERVES 4	METRIC	IMPERIAL	AMERICAN
Large prawns (jumbo shrimp)	750 g	1½ lb	1½ lb
Chilli powder	4–5 ml	¾–1 tsp	¾–1 tsp
Salt	2.5–5 ml	½–1 tsp	½–1 tsp
Juice of 1 small lemon or lime			
Oil for frying			

TO GARNISH
Lime or lemon wedges

1 Remove the heads and body shells from the prawns, but leave the tails on. Combine the chilli powder, salt and lemon or lime juice. Marinate for 1 hour.

2 Fry (sauté) for 3–4 minutes in a little hot oil. Be careful not to over cook. Serve piping hot, garnished with lemon or lime wedges.

PREPARATION TIME: 15 MINUTES PLUS MARINATING TIME
COOKING TIME: 3–4 MINUTES

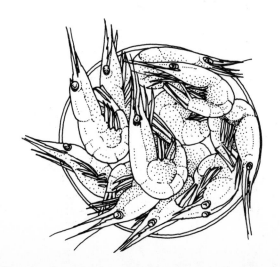

Guacamole and Salad Sticks

𝒢uacamole is a Mexican dip. You can use very ripe avocados which are often sold cheaply. You may wish to add a little more grated onion to make it go further, but this is the basic recipe.

SERVES 6	METRIC	IMPERIAL	AMERICAN
Ripe avocados	3	3	3
Onion, grated	½	½	½
Garlic cloves, crushed	2	2	2
Lemon juice	15 ml	1 tbsp	1 tbsp
Olive oil	15 ml	1 tbsp	1 tbsp
Salt and black pepper			
Cayenne	1.5 ml	¼ tsp	¼ tsp
Worcestershire sauce	1.5 ml	¼ tsp	¼ tsp
A few drops of Tabasco sauce			

TO SERVE
Mixed raw vegetables cut into sticks
(carrot, cucumber, (bell) peppers, celery, etc.)

1   In a blender or food processor, mix the flesh from the avocados with the onion and garlic until smooth. Gradually add the lemon juice and oil.

2   Season to taste with salt, black pepper, cayenne, Worcestershire and Tabasco sauce. Chill for 30 minutes.

3   Serve on individual plates with mixed raw vegetables cut into sticks.

PREPARATION TIME: 10 MINUTES PLUS CHILLING TIME

Pepper Provençale

SERVES 4	METRIC	IMPERIAL	AMERICAN
Onion, finely chopped	1	1	1
Red AND green (bell) peppers, sliced	2 each	2 each	2 each
Olive oil	30 ml	2 tbsp	2 tbsp
Garlic clove, crushed	1	1	1
Can tomatoes	400 g	14 oz	1 large
Dry white wine	45 ml	3 tbsp	3 tbsp
Sugar	5 ml	1 tsp	1 tsp
Tomato purée (paste)	15 ml	1 tbsp	1 tbsp
Herbes de Provence (OR dried mixed herbs)	5 ml	1 tsp	1 tsp
Chopped parsley	15 ml	1 tbsp	1 tbsp

TO SERVE
Crusty French bread

1   Fry (sauté) the onion and peppers in the oil until soft. Add the garlic and fry for a further 2–3 minutes.

2   Add the tomatoes, wine, sugar, tomato purée and herbs. Bring to the boil and simmer until the peppers are tender and the sauce is reduced and pulpy. Serve in ramekins (custard cups) topped with the parsley, with crusty French bread.

Note:

To make Prawn Provençale, omit the peppers, herbs and purée. Thicken the sauce with 5 ml/1 tsp cornflour (cornstarch). Add 350 g/12 oz/3 cups peeled prawns (shrimp), reheat and serve with plain boiled rice.

PREPARATION TIME: 10 MINUTES
COOKING TIME: 15 MINUTES

Smoked Mackerel Pâté

*T*his pâté is quite rich, so a little goes a long way. It also makes a delicious sandwich filling with a few crisp lettuce leaves.

SERVES 8	METRIC	IMPERIAL	AMERICAN
Smoked mackerel fillets, skinned	4	4	4
Soured (dairy sour) cream OR thick yoghurt	150 ml	¼ pt	⅔ cup
Cottage cheese	100 g	4 oz	½ cup
Juice of ½ large lemon			
Salt and pepper			
Grated nutmeg			
TO GARNISH			
Cayenne			
TO SERVE			
Hot toast			

1   Put the fish, soured cream or yoghurt, cottage cheese and lemon juice in a blender or food processor. Run the machine until well blended.

2   Season to taste with salt, pepper and nutmeg. Chill.

3   Spoon on to small plates, sprinkle with cayenne and serve with hot toast.

PREPARATION TIME: 5 MINUTES PLUS CHILLING TIME

Spanish Prawns

The chilli and almonds give an unusual spicy and nutty taste to these fried prawns. This also makes a good main course for two people, served on a bed of plain boiled rice.

SERVES 4	METRIC	IMPERIAL	AMERICAN
Butter	25 g	1 oz	2 tbsp
Olive oil	30 ml	2 tbsp	2 tbsp
Ground almonds	25 g	1 oz	¼ cup
Red chilli, finely chopped	1	1	1
Garlic clove, finely chopped	1	1	1
Peeled prawns (shrimp)	350 g	12 oz	3 cups
Rind and juice of ½ lemon			
TO GARNISH			
Chopped coriander (cilantro)	30 ml	2 tbsp	2 tbsp

1 Melt the butter in a frying pan (skillet) with the oil, add the almonds, chilli and garlic. Cook for 2 minutes.

2 Add the prawns and lemon rind and juice, and cook over a moderate heat, stirring until the prawns are heated through.

3 Spoon on to warm plates and garnish with chopped coriander.

PREPARATION TIME: 3 MINUTES
COOKING TIME: 6 MINUTES

Eggs with Tuna Fish Mayonnaise

*T*una mayonnaise is a popular Italia sauce, often served with chicken or veal, but it goes particularly well with hard-boiled (hard-cooked) eggs for an appetising starter.

SERVES 4	METRIC	IMPERIAL	AMERICAN
Can tuna	100 g	4 oz	1 small
Juice of ½ lemon			
Anchovy fillets	6	6	6
Mayonnaise	150 ml	¼ pt	⅔ cup
Black pepper			
Eggs, hard-boiled (hard-cooked), shelled	4	4	4
TO GARNISH			
Crisp lettuce leaves			
Chopped parsley			

1 Drain and mash the tuna.

2 Blend in the lemon juice. Chop and add 2 of the anchovy fillets. Place in a blender or food processor with the mayonnaise. Blend until smooth. Season to taste with pepper.

3 Cut the eggs in half lengthwise (easy with a wet knife). Arrange in pairs, rounded side up, on lettuce leaves on individual plates. Coat with the mayonnaise mixture.

4 Cut the remaining anchovies in halves lengthwise and arrange over the eggs. Sprinkle with parsley.

PREPARATION TIME: 10 MINUTES PLUS COOKING OF THE EGGS

Smoked Salmon or Trout Salad

*T*his is a great way of making a little fish go a long way and could not be simpler to make.

SERVES 4	METRIC	IMPERIAL	AMERICAN
Crisp lettuce	1	1	1
Smoked salmon OR trout, thinly sliced	50 g	2 oz	⅛ lb
Crème fraîche OR thick Greek yoghurt	40 ml	8 tsp	8 tsp
Smallest possible pot of lumpfish roe	1	1	1
Tomatoes, skinned, seeded and chopped very finely	4	4	4
Onion, finely chopped	½	½	½
Piece cucumber, finely chopped	5 cm	2 in	2 in
Stick celery, finely chopped	1	1	1

1   Cut the lettuce into thin strips and put on each plate.

2   Cut the salmon or trout into strips and arrange on the lettuce.

3   Put a spoonful of crème fraîche or Greek yoghurt in the centre and top with a little lumpfish roe.

4   Arrange the salad ingredients over the lettuce in between the fish strips and serve.

PREPARATION TIME: 8 MINUTES

Mushrooms in Cumin and Coriander Sauce

*T*his is a great standby for unexpected guests, made with canned mushrooms and UHT cream.

SERVES 2–3	METRIC	IMPERIAL	AMERICAN
Garlic clove, crushed	1	1	1
Butter	15 g	½ oz	1 tbsp
Can sliced mushrooms	298 g	10½ oz	1 small
Ground cumin	2.5 ml	½ tsp	½ tsp
Ground coriander (cilantro)	2.5 ml	½ tsp	½ tsp
Cornflour (cornstarch)	5–10 ml	1–2 tsp	1–2 tsp
UHT whipping cream	150 ml	¼ pt	⅔ cup
Salt and pepper			

TO SERVE
Hot French bread

1   Fry (sauté) the garlic in the butter for 1 minute. Add the mushrooms, cumin and coriander. Cook gently for 2 minutes.

2   Mix the cornflour and cream and add to the pan. Bring to the boil gently and simmer for 5 minutes. Taste and add more spices or cream (if too thick) and salt and pepper to taste.

3   Serve in ramekin dishes (custard cups) with hot French bread.

PREPARATION TIME: 2 MINUTES
COOKING TIME: 8 MINUTES

Piquant Mushrooms on Garlic Toasts

SERVES 6	METRIC	IMPERIAL	AMERICAN
GARLIC TOASTS			
Olive oil	30 ml	2 tbsp	2 tbsp
A pinch of dried mixed herbs			
Garlic clove, crushed	1	1	1
French bread slices	12	12	12
PIQUANT MUSHROOMS			
Olive oil	60 ml	4 tbsp	4 tbsp
Button mushrooms, halved	450 g	1 lb	1 lb
Coriander (cilantro) seeds, crushed	10 ml	2 tsp	2 tsp
Red onion, sliced	1	1	1
Red wine	90 ml	6 tbsp	6 tbsp
Red wine vinegar	15 ml	1 tbsp	1 tbsp
Clear honey	30 ml	2 tbsp	2 tbsp
TO GARNISH			
Snipped chives			

1   Prepare the toasts by mixing together the oil, herbs and garlic. Brush this over the slices of bread and toast under a hot grill (broiler) and keep warm.

2   Fry (sauté) the mushrooms, coriander and onion in the oil over a high heat for 2 minutes. Cover and cook for 2 minutes. Add the wine, vinegar and honey. Stir for 2 minutes until the sauce is reduced.

3   Spoon on to the hot toasts and serve garnished with snipped chives.

PREPARATION TIME: 10 MINUTES

COOKING TIME: 6 MINUTES

Lardon Salad

*T*his substantial salad can be varied by substituting spicy chorizo sausage for the bacon. Adding chopped hard-boiled eggs, fried almonds or avocado is also very good.

SERVES 6	METRIC	IMPERIAL	AMERICAN
Streaky bacon rashers (slices), cut in narrow strips	225 g	8 oz	½ lb
Olive oil	45 ml	3 tbsp	3 tbsp
Garlic clove, crushed	1	1	1
Red wine vinegar	15 ml	1 tbsp	1 tbsp
Mixed salad leaves	350 g	12 oz	¾ lb
Plum tomatoes, chopped	2	2	2
Spring onions (scallions), finely chopped	6	6	6
Salt and pepper			

1   Fry (sauté) the bacon pieces in the oil until nearly crisp. Add the garlic, continue cooking and, when the bacon is crisp, remove from the heat.

2   Add the vinegar and stir, then pour over the salad leaves. Season and scatter over the tomatoes and onions. Toss and serve at once.

PREPARATION TIME: 5 MINUTES
COOKING TIME: 6 MINUTES

Cajun Wings

I know it's unfashionable to eat chicken skin in these health conscious times . . . but nevertheless you must try this recipe and eat the skin, that's where the spicy taste is waiting to tickle your taste-buds. If you add a crisp green salad and baked potatoes, this recipe makes a perfect light lunch or supper for 4 people.

SERVES 8	METRIC	IMPERIAL	AMERICAN
Paprika	20 ml	4 tsp	4 tsp
Ground coriander (cilantro)	10 ml	2 tsp	2 tsp
Celery salt	5 ml	1 tsp	1 tsp
Ground cumin	5 ml	1 tsp	1 tsp
Cayenne	2.5 ml	½ tsp	½ tsp
Salt	2.5 ml	½ tsp	½ tsp
Sunflower oil	15 ml	1 tbsp	1 tbsp
Red wine vinegar	30 ml	2 tbsp	2 tbsp
Garlic clove, crushed	1	1	1
Chicken wings, wing tips removed	16	16	16
Extra oil for roasting			
TO GARNISH			
Lettuce			

1   Mix the spices together with the oil, vinegar and garlic. Rub this into the wings. Chill for at least 1 hour.

2   Place in a roasting tin (pan). Drizzle over a little extra oil and cook in the oven at 200°C/400°F/gas mark 6, for 15–20 minutes. Baste with the juices several times during cooking.

3   Serve on a bed of lettuce.

PREPARATION TIME: 10 MINUTES PLUS MARINATING TIME
COOKING TIME: 15–20 MINUTES

Fried Goat's Cheese

SERVES 8	METRIC	IMPERIAL	AMERICAN
Round goat's cheeses (size of Camemberts)	2	2	2
Apricot jam (conserve)	120 ml	4 fl oz	½ cup
Plain (all-purpose) flour	60 ml	4 tbsp	4 tbsp
Salt and pepper			
Walnuts, chopped	50 g	2 oz	½ cup
Fresh white breadcrumbs	100 g	4 oz	2 cups
Snipped chives	30 ml	2 tbsp	2 tbsp
Chopped parsley	30 ml	2 tbsp	2 tbsp
Egg, lightly beaten	1	1	1
Butter	50 g	2 oz	¼ cup
Oil	90 ml	6 tbsp	6 tbsp

TO SERVE			
Salad			

1 Spread each cheese with jam and coat with seasoned flour.

2 Mix the walnuts, breadcrumbs and herbs.

3 Dip the cheeses in the egg and then the breadcrumb mixture. Chill for at least 15 minutes.

4 Fry (sauté) the cheeses on both sides in the butter and oil until golden brown.

5 Cut into quarters and serve on a bed of salad.

PREPARATION TIME: 10 MINUTES PLUS CHILLING TIME

COOKING TIME: 5 MINUTES

Grilled Goat's Cheese Salad

*T*his grilled cheese salad is less rich than the previous fried version.

SERVES 6	METRIC	IMPERIAL	AMERICAN
Goat's cheese roll	225 g	8 oz	½ lb
Baguette slices	12	12	12
DRESSING			
Olive oil	45 ml	3 tbsp	3 tbsp
Walnut oil	45 ml	3 tbsp	3 tbsp
Balsamic vinegar	30 ml	2 tbsp	2 tbsp
Walnuts, chopped	25 g	1 oz	¼ cup
Salt and pepper			
TO GARNISH			
Crisp lettuce leaves			
Cherry tomatoes, halved	12	12	12

1   Cut the goat's cheese into 12 slices and put on top of the slices of bread. Grill (broil) for 3–4 minutes until bubbling and golden.

2   Meanwhile, mix together the salad dressing ingredients. Serve two hot toasts on each plate surrounded by the lettuce and tomatoes with the dressing drizzled over.

PREPARATION TIME: 8 MINUTES
COOKING TIME: 3–4 MINUTES

Main Courses

*D*inner parties should be a pleasure for the cook as well as the guests. All these main courses are simple to make. Most can be prepared in advance, then just finished at the last minute. When planning your menu, it's usually best to choose the main course first, then a starter and pudding to compliment it.

Chicken with Piquant Caper Relish

*T*he relish (salsa verde) makes this simple fried chicken taste and look really special.

SERVES 6	METRIC	IMPERIAL	AMERICAN
Anchovy fillets, drained of their oil	3	3	3
Garlic cloves, crushed	2	2	2
Balsamic vinegar	2.5 ml	½ tsp	½ tsp
Capers	15 ml	1 tbsp	1 tbsp
Chopped parsley	60 ml	4 tbsp	4 tbsp
Olive oil	150 ml	¼ pt	⅔ cup
Pepper			
Chicken breast fillets	6 × 175 g	6 × 6 oz	6 × ⅓ lb
Unsalted (sweet) butter	25 g	1 oz	2 tbsp
Sunflower oil	15 ml	1 tbsp	1 tbsp

TO SERVE
Sautéed potatoes, broccoli and carrots

1   Purée the first five ingredients in a blender or food processor until well combined.

2   Gradually add the olive oil, running the machine all the time, and season with pepper.

3   Fry (sauté) the chicken breasts in the butter and oil for 5–6 minutes on each side until cooked through.

4   Serve each with a spoonful of the salsa, accompanied by sautéed potatoes, broccoli and carrots.

PREPARATION TIME: 10 MINUTES
COOKING TIME: 5–6 MINUTES

Chicken in Pesto Sauce

*T*his recipe shows that economical ingredients can combine to make a delectable dish.

SERVES 4	METRIC	IMPERIAL	AMERICAN
Chicken breast fillets	4	4	4
Plain (all-purpose) flour	15 ml	1 tbsp	1 tbsp
Olive oil	30 ml	2 tbsp	2 tbsp
Onion, chopped	1	1	1
Button mushrooms	100 g	4 oz	¼ lb
Tomatoes, skinned and chopped	5	5	5
Medium dry white wine	300 ml	½ pt	1¼ cups
Tomato purée (paste)	15 ml	1 tbsp	1 tbsp
Pesto (see page 157)	30 ml	2 tbsp	2 tbsp
Chopped parsley	60 ml	4 tbsp	4 tbsp
Salt and pepper			

TO SERVE		
Baked Sliced Potatoes and Courgette Patties (see pages 135 and 128)		

1 Coat the chicken in the flour and fry (sauté) in the oil until golden brown. Remove from the pan and keep warm.

2 Fry the onion for 5 minutes and then add the mushrooms, tomatoes, wine and tomato purée. Bring to the boil, then simmer for 15 minutes.

3 Return the chicken to the pan, add the pesto and parsley and season to taste. Cook for 5 minutes. Serve with Baked Sliced Potatoes and Courgette Patties.

PREPARATION TIME: 10 MINUTES
COOKING TIME: 30 MINUTES

Chicken with Tarragon Cream

*T*his sumptuous chicken dish has a sophisticated and delicate flavour, yet is quick and easy to prepare.

SERVES 4	METRIC	IMPERIAL	AMERICAN
Boneless chicken breasts	4	4	4
Unsalted (sweet) butter	25 g	1 oz	2 tbsp
Plain (all-purpose) flour	10 ml	2 tsp	2 tsp
Salt	2.5 ml	½ tsp	½ tsp
Black pepper	1.5 ml	¼ tsp	¼ tsp
Dried tarragon	2.5 ml	½ tsp	½ tsp
French mustard	5 ml	1 tsp	1 tsp
White wine	120 ml	4 fl oz	½ cup
Double (heavy) cream	120 ml	4 fl oz	½ cup

TO SERVE
Mustard Roast Potatoes, Buttered Carrots and Parsley and Fried Peas with Garlic (see pages 130, 126 and 146)

1   Fry (sauté) the chicken breasts in the butter for about 20 minutes until cooked through, then remove from the pan and keep warm.

2   Add the flour, salt and pepper, tarragon and mustard to the pan. Gradually pour in the wine, stirring all the time. Bring to the boil and let it bubble until reduced by half.

3   Add the cream, chicken breasts and any juices. Cook for a further 5–6 minutes over a gentle heat. Serve with Mustard Roast Potatoes, Buttered Carrots and Parsley and Fried Peas with Garlic.

PREPARATION TIME: 5 MINUTES
COOKING TIME: 30 MINUTES

Fragrant Cardamom Chicken

SERVES 4	METRIC	IMPERIAL	AMERICAN
Boneless chicken breasts	4	4	4
Salt and pepper			
Butter	50 g	2 oz	¼ cup
Green (bell) pepper, sliced	1	1	1
Green cardamoms, crushed	8	8	8
Sweet white vermouth	150 ml	¼ pt	⅔ cup
Marmite (yeast extract)	5 ml	1 tsp	1 tsp
Double (heavy) cream	300 ml	½ pt	1¼ cups

TO GARNISH
Watercress

TO SERVE
Mushrooms in butter, sweetcorn (corn) and boiled rice

1   Season chicken with the salt and pepper, then fry (sauté) for 20 minutes in the butter until cooked through. Remove from the pan and keep warm.

2   Fry the sliced pepper and cardamom seeds in the chicken juices until the pepper is softening. Pour in the vermouth and stir to scrape up any sediment. Cook over a moderate heat for about 10 minutes until well reduced, add the Marmite and cream and cook until thickened (about 5 minutes).

3   Serve the chicken pieces with the sauce poured over, garnished with the watercress and accompanied with mushrooms fried in butter, sweetcorn and boiled rice.

PREPARATION TIME: 5 MINUTES
COOKING TIME: 40 MINUTES

Oriental Marinated Pork or Chicken

*A*lthough this marinade is suitable for both pork and chicken, I think it is perfect for pork as it imparts juiciness as well as flavour to the meat. After marinating, the meat can be cooked on the barbecue instead of in the oven.

SERVES 6	METRIC	IMPERIAL	AMERICAN
Soy sauce	45 ml	3 tbsp	3 tbsp
Clear honey	45 ml	3 tbsp	3 tbsp
Juice of 2 oranges			
Garlic clove, crushed	1	1	1
Fresh root ginger (ginger root), finely chopped	15 ml	1 tbsp	1 tbsp
Soft brown sugar	10 ml	2 tsp	2 tsp
Sunflower oil	75 ml	5 tbsp	5 tbsp
Ground cumin	5 ml	1 tsp	1 tsp
Pork chops, pork steaks or chicken breasts	6	6	6
TO SERVE			
Stir-fried Vegetables (see page 135)			

1 Mix together the first eight ingredients and pour over the meat. Leave to marinate for several hours or overnight, if possible, turning over occasionally.

2 Bake in the oven at 180°C/350°F/gas mark 4 for 45 minutes. This is delicious served with Stir-fried Vegetables.

PREPARATION TIME: 5 MINUTES PLUS MARINATING TIME

COOKING TIME: 45 MINUTES

Melting Moments Chicken Cordon Bleu

A wonderfully moist version of a chicken dish which is often cooked under the grill (broiler).

SERVES 4	METRIC	IMPERIAL	AMERICAN
Chicken breasts, boned and skinned	4	4	4
Butter and oil for frying			
Chopped parsley	15 ml	1 tbsp	1 tbsp
Slices ham	4	4	4
Mushrooms, sliced	8	8	8
Chicken stock	150 ml	¼ pt	⅔ cup
Slices quick-melting cheese	4	4	4
TO SERVE			
Roast potatoes, sweetcorn (corn) and broccoli			

1 Fry (sauté) the chicken in a little butter and oil on each side to brown.

2 Top each with a little parsley, a slice of ham and sliced mushrooms.

3 Add the chicken stock. Cover and simmer until cooked through.

4 Top each breast with a slice of cheese. Cover again and cook until the cheese melts.

5 Serve with roast potatoes, sweetcorn and broccoli.

PREPARATION TIME: 5 MINUTES	
COOKING TIME: 30 MINUTES	

Boozy Chicken

SERVES 4	METRIC	IMPERIAL	AMERICAN
Chicken breasts, boned and skinned	4	4	4
Salt and pepper			
Butter	50 g	2 oz	¼ cup
Onions, sliced	100 g	4 oz	1 cup
Garlic clove, chopped	1	1	1
Can tomatoes	200 g	8 oz	small
Port or sherry	75 ml	5 tbsp	5 tbsp
Dried basil	10 ml	2 tsp	2 tsp
Chopped parsley	60 ml	4 tbsp	4 tbsp
Soft brown sugar	5 ml	1 tsp	1 tsp

TO SERVE
Baked Sliced Potatoes, Thyme and Parsley Carrots and Fried Peas with Garlic (see pages 135, 126 and 146)

1   Rub the chicken breasts with salt and pepper and fry (sauté) in half the butter for 30 minutes until cooked through.

2   In a separate pan, cook the onion in the remaining butter for 5 minutes, adding the garlic after 2–3 minutes. Add the tomatoes and cook for 10 minutes.

3   Stir the port, sherry, basil, parsley and sugar into the tomato mixture and bring to the boil. Add the chicken, reduce heat, cover and simmer for 10 minutes.

4   Serve with Baked Sliced Potatoes, Thyme and Parsley Carrots and Fried Peas with Garlic.

PREPARATION TIME: 5 MINUTES

COOKING TIME: 55 MINUTES

Three-spice Turkey

*B*oth pork steaks and chicken breasts work just as well as turkey in this spicy dish.

SERVES 4	METRIC	IMPERIAL	AMERICAN
Unsalted (sweet) butter	75 g	3 oz	⅓ cup
Spring onions (scallions), finely chopped	4	4	4
Plain (all-purpose) flour	25 g	1 oz	¼ cup
White wine	150 ml	¼ pt	⅔ cup
Water	300 ml	½ pt	1¼ cups
Ground cumin	15 ml	1 tbsp	1 tbsp
Ground cardamom	15 ml	1 tbsp	1 tbsp
Ground coriander (cilantro)	30 ml	2 tbsp	2 tbsp
Garlic clove, crushed	1	1	1
Salt and pepper			
Turkey escalopes	4	4	4
Seasoned flour	30 ml	2 tbsp	2 tbsp
Double (heavy) cream	150 ml	¼ pt	⅔ cup

TO SERVE			
Artichoke and Potato Bake (see page 147) and broccoli			

1   Fry (sauté) the spring onions in half the butter until soft, then stir in the flour and cook for a further minute.

2   Add the wine, water, spices, garlic, salt and pepper and cook for a further 10–15 minutes until slightly thickened.

3   Meanwhile, toss the turkey escalopes in seasoned flour and fry in a separate pan in the remaining butter. When browned on both sides (after about 5–10 minutes), pour the other mixture over and continue to cook for 5 minutes.

4   Add the cream and simmer for another 5 minutes. Serve with Artichoke and Potato Bake and broccoli.

PREPARATION TIME: 5 MINUTES

COOKING TIME: 30–35 MINUTES

Turkey Escalopes in Ginger Wine

*G*inger wine makes a rich and delicious sauce – try it with chicken or veal too.

SERVES 8	METRIC	IMPERIAL	AMERICAN
Escalopes of turkey	8	8	8
Olive oil	30 ml	2 tbsp	2 tbsp
Unsalted (sweet) butter	100 g	4 oz	½ cup
Ginger wine	300 ml	½ pt	1¼ cups
Lemon juice	20 ml	4 tsp	4 tsp
Stem ginger, chopped	10 ml	2 tsp	2 tsp
Double (heavy) cream	90 ml	6 tbsp	6 tbsp
Salt and pepper			

TO SERVE
Roast potatoes, carrots and buttered green beans

1 Gently fry (sauté) the escalopes in the oil and butter for 5–6 minutes. Lift on to a serving dish and keep warm.

2 Add the ginger wine to the pan and bring to the boil. Simmer for 5 minutes until the wine is syrupy.

3 Stir in the lemon juice, stem ginger and cream. Simmer for 2–3 minutes until the sauce is a pale coffee colour. Season with salt and pepper.

4 Pour the sauce over the meat and serve with roast potatoes, carrots and buttered green beans.

PREPARATION TIME: 5 MINUTES
COOKING TIME: 15 MINUTES

Fillet of Turkey with Vermouth

*T*his fresh-tasting supper dish is equally delicious with chicken or pork fillet.

SERVES 2	METRIC	IMPERIAL	AMERICAN
Turkey escalopes	2	2	2
Flour	15–30 ml	1–2 tbsp	1–2 tbsp
Salt and pepper			
Butter	50 g	2 oz	¼ cup
Stock	60 ml	4 tbsp	4 tbsp
Dry vermouth	60 ml	4 tbsp	4 tbsp
Spring onion (scallion), chopped	1	1	1
Sprig of parsley, chopped	1	1	1
A pinch of chopped rosemary			
Small lemon, very thinly sliced	¼	¼	¼

TO SERVE
Buttered new potatoes, broccoli and carrots

1 Slice the turkey into narrow strips, season the flour with salt and pepper and dust the meat lightly with it.

2 Quickly fry (sauté) the strips in the butter, then add the stock and vermouth. Boil rapidly until slightly thickened.

3 Scatter the spring onion and parsley over the meat with the rosemary. Add the lemon slices and cook for a further 2–3 minutes.

4 Serve with buttered new potatoes, broccoli and carrots.

PREPARATION TIME: 10 MINUTES
COOKING TIME: 8 MINUTES

Peppered Duck Breasts

*D*uck breasts are a rich, dense meat so they are more economical than you think as a small amount satisfies even the healthiest appetite!

SERVES 6	METRIC	IMPERIAL	AMERICAN
Cracked black peppercorns	90 ml	6 tbsp	6 tbsp
Small duck breasts, skin removed	6	6	6
Salt			
Sunflower oil	45 ml	3 tbsp	3 tbsp
Unsalted (sweet) butter	45 ml	3 tbsp	3 tbsp
Cognac	300 ml	½ pt	1¼ cups
Duck or chicken stock	300 ml	½ pt	1¼ cups
Double (heavy) cream	300 ml	½ pt	1¼ cups

TO SERVE
Creamed Spinach, Antibes Potatoes (see pages 136 and 133) and fried mushrooms

1 Press the peppercorns into the duck and season with a little salt.

2 Fry (sauté) in the oil and butter for 4–5 minutes on each side. Remove from the pan and keep warm.

3 De-glaze the pan with the cognac and stock. Stirring well, bring to the boil and reduce the liquid by half. Add the cream and heat gently. Serve with Creamed Spinach, Antibes Potatoes and fried mushrooms.

PREPARATION TIME: 5 MINUTES
COOKING TIME: 15 MINUTES

Sautéed Duck with Port

SERVES 4	METRIC	IMPERIAL	AMERICAN
Large duck breasts	2	2	2
Port	90 ml	6 tbsp	6 tbsp
Redcurrant jelly (clear conserve)	15 ml	1 tbsp	1 tbsp
Salt and pepper			
TO GARNISH			
Sprigs of watercress			
TO SERVE			
Creamed Spinach and Mustard Roast Potatoes (see pages 136 and 130)			

1   Sprinkle a frying pan (skillet) with salt, add the duck skin-side down. Cook gently for 5 minutes. Turn over and cook for 5 minutes more. Remove from the pan and keep warm, skin-side up.

2   Add the port, boil to reduce by half. Stir in the redcurrant jelly until dissolved. Season.

3   Cut the duck into chunky slices, add to the sauce. If the slices are too rare for your taste, cook for another minute. Taste the sauce. If it is too sweet or thick, add a little more port. Garnish with watercress and serve with Creamed Spinach and Mustard Roast Potatoes.

PREPARATION TIME: 2 MINUTES
COOKING TIME: 15 MINUTES

Pork Chops with Orange Sauce

SERVES 4	METRIC	IMPERIAL	AMERICAN
Pork chops	4	4	4
Oil	15 ml	1 tbsp	1 tbsp
Salt and black pepper			
White wine	150 ml	¼ pt	⅔ cup
Cornflour (cornstarch)	6.5 ml	1¼ tsp	1¼ tsp
Ground cinnamon	1.5 ml	¼ tsp	¼ tsp
Orange juice	250 ml	8 fl oz	1 cup
Orange, rind grated and flesh sliced	1	1	1
Cloves	4	4	4

TO SERVE

Turkish Fried Carrots and Mustard Roast Potatoes
(see pages 125 and 130)

1   Fry (sauté) the chops in the oil for about 4 minutes on each side. Add salt, pepper and the wine, cover and simmer for about 30 minutes.

2   Meanwhile, mix together the cornflour, cinnamon, half the orange juice, the rind and also the slices of orange.

3   Remove the chops and keep warm. Add the remaining orange juice to the pan with the cloves and cook until reduced by half, then remove the cloves and add the cornflour mixture. Boil for 2 minutes, stirring.

4   Pour the sauce over the chops and serve with Turkish Fried Carrots and Mustard Roast Potatoes.

PREPARATION TIME: 5 MINUTES

COOKING TIME: 40 MINUTES

Spiced Pork with Cider

SERVES 3–4	METRIC	IMPERIAL	AMERICAN
Pork fillet (or chicken)	450 g	1 lb	1 lb
A good pinch of ground ginger			
A good pinch of mixed (apple-pie) spice			
A good pinch of cayenne			
Onion, thinly sliced	½	½	½
Green (bell) pepper, thinly sliced	1	1	1
Oil	30 ml	2 tbsp	2 tbsp
Unsalted (sweet) butter	50 g	2 oz	¼ cup
Button mushrooms, quartered	175 g	6 oz	3 cups
Cider	150 ml	¼ pt	⅔ cup
Double (heavy) cream	150 ml	¼ pt	⅔ cup
Salt and pepper			

TO SERVE
Stir-fried Vegetables (see page 135) and noodles

1   Cut the pork fillet into 5 mm/¼ in slices, then into thin strips and dust with the spices.

2   Gently fry (sauté) the onion and pepper in the oil and butter until softened. Increase the heat and add the pork and mushrooms. Cook for 5 minutes, then pour in the cider and cook until reduced slightly.

3   Lower the heat and blend in the cream. Reheat slowly for about 5–10 minutes until thickened. Season.

4   Serve with Stir-fried Vegetables and noodles.

PREPARATION TIME: 10 MINUTES
COOKING TIME: 20 MINUTES

Rolled Pork Slices

SERVES 6	METRIC	IMPERIAL	AMERICAN
Slices of pork fillet	6	6	6
Salt and pepper			
Raw cured ham (Westphalian, Parma, Serrano, etc.), chopped	100 g	4 oz	1 cup
Pine nuts, chopped	25 g	1 oz	¼ cup
Sultanas (golden raisins), chopped	50 g	2 oz	⅓ cup
Fresh breadcrumbs	45 ml	3 tbsp	3 tbsp
Capers, rinsed and dried	50 g	2 oz	½ cup
Olive oil	45 ml	3 tbsp	3 tbsp
White wine	30 ml	2 tbsp	2 tbsp
Passata (sieved tomatoes)	45 ml	3 tbsp	3 tbsp
Green chilli, seeded and finely chopped	1	1	1

TO SERVE
Pasta and fried (sautéed) courgettes (zucchini)

1   Beat the pork slices until very thin. Season.

2   Mix together the ham, nuts, sultanas, breadcrumbs and capers and spoon on to the pork.

3   Roll up and secure with cocktail sticks (tooth picks). Brown the rolls in the olive oil.

4   Add the wine, passata and chilli. Simmer gently for 2 hours. Serve with pasta and fried courgettes.

PREPARATION TIME: 15 MINUTES
COOKING TIME: 2 HOURS

Mediterranean Baked Pork

If you are feeling lazy, you can use a ready-made pasta sauce in place of this tomato sauce.

SERVES 6	METRIC	IMPERIAL	AMERICAN
Pork fillets, trimmed	750 g	1½ lb	1½ lb
Eggs, beaten	2	2	2
Grated Parmesan cheese	75 g	3 oz	¾ cup
Plain (all-purpose) flour	50 g	2 oz	½ cup
Oil	30 ml	2 tbsp	2 tbsp
Onions, chopped	2	2	2
Garlic clove, crushed	1	1	1
Bacon rashers (slices), rinded	4	4	4
Can tomatoes	400 g	14 oz	1 large
Tomato purée (paste)	50 g	2 oz	¼ cup
A dash of Worcestershire sauce			
Dried mixed herbs	5 ml	1 tsp	1 tsp
Chicken stock	250 ml	8 fl oz	1 cup
Salt and pepper			
Cayenne			
Cheddar cheese, grated	75 g	3 oz	¾ cup

TO SERVE
Baked potatoes and a crunchy green salad

1   Cut the pork fillets into chunks and dip in the egg.

2   Mix half the Parmesan with the flour and use to coat the meat, then fry (sauté) the chunks in half of the oil.

3   Meanwhile, chop the bacon and fry it with the onions and garlic in the remaining oil. When the onions are soft, add the tomatoes, tomato purée, Worcestershire sauce, herbs and stock. Season to taste with a little salt, pepper and cayenne. Cook for about 10 minutes.

4   Layer the meat and sauce in a casserole dish (Dutch oven) and before adding the last layer of sauce sprinkle the grated Cheddar over. Cover with the last layer of sauce and then top with the remaining Parmesan. Bake for 1¼ hours at 190°C/375°F/gas mark 5.

5   Serve with baked potatoes and a crunchy green salad.

PREPARATION TIME: 15 MINUTES

COOKING TIME: 1½ HOURS

Pork Tenderloin with Mushrooms

*T*his is very easy to cook, but extra time is needed for marinating. I like to marinate the meat overnight, but when time is short, 30 minutes would give the meat a definitive flavour.

SERVES 6	METRIC	IMPERIAL	AMERICAN
Pork tenderloin	750 g	1½ lb	1½ lb
Oil	30 ml	2 tbsp	2 tbsp
Lemon juice	15 ml	1 tbsp	1 tbsp
Black pepper			
Garlic clove, crushed	1	1	1
SAUCE			
Unsalted (sweet) butter	50 g	2 oz	¼ cup
Onion, finely sliced	1	1	1
Button mushrooms, finely sliced	175 g	6 oz	3 cups
Dry sherry	30 ml	2 tbsp	2 tbsp
Salt and pepper			
Double (heavy) cream	150 ml	¼ pt	⅔ cup
TO SERVE			
Plain boiled rice and a crisp green salad			

1   Cut the meat into 2 cm/¾ in slices. Lay them between cling film (plastic wrap) or greaseproof (waxed) paper and beat flat with a rolling pin. Arrange the slices in a shallow dish.

2   Mix the oil and lemon juice, season with black pepper, add the garlic and spoon this marinade over the meat. Leave for a minimum of 30 minutes or preferably overnight, turning occasionally, if possible.

3 Melt the butter and fry (sauté) the onions until soft but not brown.

4 Add the mushrooms and fry for 3 minutes. Remove from the pan with a draining spoon and keep warm.

5 Drain the pork from the marinade and fry gently in the pan for 3–4 minutes, turning once. Transfer to a serving dish and keep warm.

6 Add the sherry to the pan and heat until it reduces by half. Return the onions and mushrooms to the pan with salt and pepper to taste. Stir in the cream and heat gently. Remove from the heat and pour over the pork.

7 Serve surrounded by boiled rice with a crisp green salad.

PREPARATION TIME: 10 MINUTES PLUS MARINATING TIME

COOKING TIME: 15 MINUTES

Nutty-topped Pork

*T*his is quite a versatile recipe as you can use pork chops or steaks or, better still, slices of tenderloin. Also you can either grill (broil) or fry (sauté) and then bake the meat. The choice is yours, depending on how many guests you have.

SERVES 8	METRIC	IMPERIAL	AMERICAN
Pork chops or steaks	8	8	8
Mustard powder	20 ml	4 tsp	4 tsp
Soft brown sugar	45 ml	3 tbsp	3 tbsp
Salted peanuts, chopped	30 ml	2 tbsp	2 tbsp
Worcestershire sauce	10 ml	2 tsp	2 tsp
Wine vinegar	10 ml	2 tsp	2 tsp
Salt	5 ml	1 tsp	1 tsp
Butter, melted	10 ml	2 tsp	2 tsp

TO SERVE
French beans in a tomato sauce, Baked Sliced Potatoes (see pages 158 and 135) and carrots

1   Grill (broil) or fry (sauté) the pork until nearly cooked.

2   Mix all the other ingredients together and spread over the chops. Grill until they are golden brown. Or you can bake in the oven at 200°C/400°F/gas mark 6 for about 20 minutes just until the topping is golden brown.

3   Serve with French beans in a tomato sauce, Baked Sliced Potatoes and carrots.

PREPARATION TIME: 5 MINUTES
COOKING TIME: 30 MINUTES

Herby Roast Pork with Cream Sauce

SERVES 6	METRIC	IMPERIAL	AMERICAN
Dried mixed herbs	5 ml	1 tsp	1 tsp
Pork loin, skinned, boned and rolled	1.5 kg	3 lb	3 lb
A little oil			
Salt and pepper			
Sweet white vermouth	60 ml	4 tbsp	4 tbsp
Vegetable stock cube	1	1	1
Single (light) cream	150 ml	¼ pt	⅔ cup

TO SERVE
Mustard Roast Potatoes, Garlicky French Beans and Buttered Carrots with Parsley (see pages 130, 144 and 126)

1   Sprinkle the herbs over the pork. Place on a trivet in a roasting tin (pan). Roast at 220°C/425°F/gas mark 7 for about 1½–2 hours until cooked through. Remove the meat from the tin and let it rest until ready to carve.

2   Make the sauce. Pour off the fat from the tin, add the vermouth and stock cube. Bring to the boil, stirring constantly.

3   Add the cream and continue to heat gently. If too thick, add a little water, and if too thin add some cornflour (cornstarch) mixed with a little more cream.

4   Carve the meat and serve with Mustard Roast Potatoes, Garlicky French Beans and Buttered Carrots with Parsley.

PREPARATION TIME: 10 MINUTES
COOKING TIME: 1¾–2¼ HOURS

Spanish Pork Stew

*T*his is a filling and hearty (but not heavy) stew and can be cooked either in the oven or on the hob.

SERVES 4	METRIC	IMPERIAL	AMERICAN
Butter	75 g	3 oz	⅓ cup
Olive oil	45 ml	3 tbsp	3 tbsp
Pork shoulder, cubed	900 g	2 lb	2 lb
Salt and pepper			
Spanish onion, thinly sliced	1	1	1
Garlic cloves, thinly sliced	2	2	2
Green (bell) pepper, sliced	1	1	1
Mushrooms, sliced	100 g	4 oz	2 cups
Can tomatoes	400 g	14 oz	1 large
Dry white wine	225 ml	8 fl oz	1 cup
Dried oregano	10 ml	2 tsp	2 tsp
Dried rosemary	5 ml	1 tsp	1 tsp
Grated rind of 1 lemon			
Salt and pepper			
Courgettes (zucchini), sliced	450 g	1 lb	4 cups
TO SERVE			
Garlic bread			

1   Use a third of the butter and two thirds of the oil to fry (sauté) the pork until lightly browned. Set the meat aside.

2   To the fat still in the pan, add half the remaining butter and all the remaining olive oil. Add the onion, garlic and green pepper and fry for 8–9 minutes. Stir in the mushrooms and the can of tomatoes and cook for 3–4 minutes.

3   Add the wine, oregano, rosemary and lemon rind, and season with salt and pepper. Bring to the boil and stir to remove any sediment on the pan sides, then add the meat.

4 Bring back to the boil, reduce the heat, cover and simmer for 2 hours, or cook in the oven for 2 hours at 160°C/325°F/gas mark 3.

5 Meanwhile, fry the courgettes in the remaining butter until lightly coloured but not too soft. Add to the stew 5 minutes before serving. No extra vegetables are necessary, but serve with garlic bread.

PREPARATION TIME: 10 MINUTES
COOKING TIME: 2¼ HOURS

Pork and Apricot Casserole

*T*his casserole can be cooked in a slow cooker for 6–7 hours or the ordinary oven for 2 hours as shown below.

SERVES 4	METRIC	IMPERIAL	AMERICAN
Onion, chopped	1	1	1
Rashers (slices) bacon, chopped	2	2	2
Butter	25 g	1 oz	2 tbsp
Stewing pork, diced	750 g	1½ lb	1½ lb
Seasoned flour	25 g	1 oz	2 tbsp
Tomato purée (paste)	30 ml	2 tbsp	2 tbsp
White wine	300 ml	½ pt	1¼ cups
Chicken stock cube	1	1	1
Dried apricots, chopped	50 g	2 oz	⅓ cup

TO SERVE
Plain boiled rice and green beans or broccoli

1   Fry (sauté) the onion and bacon in the butter for 2–3 minutes.

2   Toss the pork in the seasoned flour and brown in the pan.

3   Add the tomato purée, wine, stock cube and apricots, stirring until thickened.

4   Transfer to a casserole (Dutch oven) and cook in the oven at 160°C/325°F/gas mark 3 for 2–2½ hours.

5   Serve with rice and green beans or broccoli.

PREPARATION TIME: 10 MINUTES
COOKING TIME: 2½ HOURS

Cidered Pork Fillet

I use the microwave on low where the recipe says use the oven which makes this even quicker. It can be reheated and served later very successfully.

SERVES 4	METRIC	IMPERIAL	AMERICAN
Pork tenderloin	750 g	1½ lb	1½ lb
Butter	15 g	½ oz	1 tbsp
Olive oil	30 ml	2 tbsp	2 tbsp
Onion, chopped	1	1	1
Red (bell) pepper, sliced	1	1	1
Ground coriander (cilantro)	15 ml	1 tbsp	1 tbsp
Plain (all-purpose) flour	15 g	½ oz	1 tbsp
Dry cider	300 ml	½ pt	1¼ cups
Vegetable stock	150 ml	¼ pt	⅔ cup
Chopped fresh coriander			

TO SERVE
Rice, green beans and sweetcorn (corn)

1   Cut the pork in 1 cm/½ in slices and beat flat with a rolling pin between cling film (plastic wrap) or greaseproof (waxed) paper. Fry (sauté) in the butter and 15 ml/1 tbsp of the oil for 2 minutes on each side. Transfer to a casserole (Dutch oven).

2   Fry the onion in the remaining oil for 1 minute, add the red pepper and cook for 3–4 minutes.

3   Stir in the ground coriander, flour, cider and stock. Bring to the boil and add to the casserole. Cook for 30 minutes at 180°C/350°F/gas mark 4, adding the fresh coriander for the last 15 minutes. Serve with rice, green beans and sweetcorn.

PREPARATION TIME: 15 MINUTES
COOKING TIME: 55 MINUTES

Spiced Beef Casserole

SERVES 4	METRIC	IMPERIAL	AMERICAN
Stewing beef, cubed	750 g	1½ lb	1½ lb
Button mushrooms	175 g	6 oz	⅓ lb
Sunflower oil	30 ml	2 tbsp	2 tbsp
Plain (all-purpose) flour	40 g	1½ oz	3 tbsp
Beef stock	300 ml	½ pt	1¼ cups
Orange juice	300 ml	½ pt	1¼ cups
White wine vinegar	10 ml	2 tsp	2 tsp
Brown sugar	10 ml	2 tsp	2 tsp
Ground cinnamon	2.5 ml	½ tsp	½ tsp
Bouquet garni	1	1	1
Grated rind of ½ an orange			
Salt and black pepper			
Rum	15 ml	1 tbsp	1 tbsp

TO SERVE
Broccoli and Potato Bake and Thyme and Parsley Carrots (see pages 148 and 126)

1   Fry (sauté) the meat and mushrooms in the oil until brown. Add the flour and cook for 1 minute.

2   Blend in the stock and orange juice. Stir in the remaining ingredients. Bring to the boil, cover and cook in the oven at 180°C/350°F/gas mark 4 for 2½ hours.

3   Remove the bouquet garni and re-season. Serve with Broccoli and Potato Bake and Thyme and Parsley Carrots.

PREPARATION TIME: 10 MINUTES

COOKING TIME: 2 HOURS 35 MINUTES

Steak Madeira

*T*he madeira sauce gives a new dimension to classic fillet steaks and the addition of mixed peppercorns imparts a subtle piquancy.

SERVES 2	METRIC	IMPERIAL	AMERICAN
Fillet steaks	2 × 175 g	2 × 6 oz	2 × ⅓ lb
Mixed peppercorns (green, pink and black)	7.5 ml	1½ tsp	1½ tsp
Sunflower oil	30 ml	2 tbsp	2 tbsp
Shallots, chopped	2	2	2
Madeira	60 ml	4 tbsp	4 tbsp
Salt			
Butter	25 g	1 oz	2 tbsp

TO SERVE
Creamy Courgette Bake (see page 127) and buttered new potatoes

1   Lightly score the steaks, crush the peppercorns and press into the surfaces. Fry (sauté) them in the oil, for between 5 and 10 minutes depending on your taste, turning once. Remove from the pan and keep warm while you make the sauce.

2   Add all the other ingredients plus 90 ml/6 tbsp water. Bring to the boil, stirring occasionally, and let it boil until slightly reduced. Check the seasoning.

3   Serve the steaks with the sauce spooned over with Creamy Courgette Bake and buttered new potatoes.

PREPARATION TIME: 5 MINUTES
COOKING TIME: 10–12 MINUTES

Carpaccio con Salsa Verde

*C*arpaccio is an Italian recipe where the beef is marinated and often not cooked at all. However, here it is given a quick blast in a very hot oven which is all it needs. Don't over cook!

SERVES 6	METRIC	IMPERIAL	AMERICAN
THE CARPACCIO			
Fillet of beef	450 g	1 lb	1 lb
Olive oil	90 ml	6 tbsp	6 tbsp
Soy sauce	30 ml	2 tbsp	2 tbsp
Black pepper			
THE SALSA			
Anchovy fillets, drained of their oil	3	3	3
Garlic cloves, crushed	2	2	2
Balsamic vinegar	2.5 ml	½ tsp	½ tsp
Capers	15 ml	1 tbsp	1 tbsp
Chopped parsley	60 ml	4 tbsp	4 tbsp
Olive oil	150 ml	¼ pt	⅔ cup
Pepper			
TO SERVE			
Pasta with Vegetable Ribbons and Soy Garlic Beans (see pages 140 and 151)			

1   The beef has to be sliced really thinly and I have found the best way to do this is to freeze it until it's fairly solid, then you can slice it quite easily with a sharp knife. Put the thin slices under cling film (plastic wrap) and beat them with a rolling pin or meat mallet so they are nearly transparent.

2   Mix together the olive oil, soy sauce and plenty of black pepper and pour this marinade over the meat. Leave for a minimum of 2 hours, but preferably overnight. Turn the meat over occasionally, if possible, to ensure even coating with the marinade.

3   Meanwhile make the salsa by puréeing all the ingredients, except the oil, in a blender or food processor. Gradually add the oil, running the machine all the time, and season with pepper.

4   Lay the drained beef slices on 2 large baking sheets (it must be a single layer only). Bake in a very hot oven 240°C/ 475°F/gas mark 9 for between 1 and 2 minutes until the slices are just turning brown.

5   Serve immediately on warmed plates dressed with a little of the salsa. Pasta with Vegetable Ribbons and Soy Garlic Beans are perfect accompaniments to this unusual dish.

PREPARATION TIME: 10 MINUTES, PLUS FREEZING AND
     MARINATING TIME

COOKING TIME: 2 MINUTES

Redcurrant Beef

*O*ne of the advantages of this recipe is that you can partly
cook the beef in advance. To do this simply brown the
meat and follow the instructions up to the point when you
have seasoned the sauce after adding the redcurrant jelly, but
do not keep the meat warm. Later replace the meat and finish
the recipe. The taste of beef cooked like this is rich and fruity
and amazingly tender.

SERVES 6	METRIC	IMPERIAL	AMERICAN
Pink peppercorns (or plenty of coarse ground black pepper)	20	20	20
Beef fillet, cut into 6 even slices	600 g	1¼ lb	1¼ lb
Oil	30 ml	2 tbsp	2 tbsp
Shallots, finely chopped	5	5	5
Streaky bacon rashers (slices), rinded and cut into strips	50 g	2 oz	2 oz
Smoked bacon rashers (slices), rinded and cut into strips	50 g	2 oz	2 oz
Red wine	175 ml	6 fl oz	¾ cup
Beef stock	50 ml	2 fl oz	3½ tbsp
Lemon juice	15 ml	1 tbsp	1 tbsp
A good pinch of ground nutmeg			
Redcurrant jelly (clear conserve)	30 ml	2 tbsp	2 tbsp
Salt and pepper			
TO SERVE			
Creamed Spinach (see page 136) and pasta with butter and thyme			

1   Lightly crush the pink peppercorns if using. Sprinkle on
both sides of the beef slices.

2   Heat the oil and seal the beef on each side. When browned remove from the pan and keep warm.

3   Add the shallots and bacon pieces to the pan and sauté for 4–5 minutes.

4   Mix in the wine, stock, lemon juice and nutmeg. Bring to the boil, stir in the redcurrant jelly until dissolved and season.

5   Replace the meat and simmer for about 5–10 minutes until the meat is tender.

6   Serve with Creamed Spinach and tagliatelle to which you have added butter, black pepper and a little chopped thyme (if you only have dried thyme, then add this to the water in which you are going to boil the pasta).

PREPARATION TIME: 10 MINUTES

COOKING TIME: 15 MINUTES

Creamy Mushroom Steaks

SERVES 4	METRIC	IMPERIAL	AMERICAN
Onion, finely chopped	1	1	1
Olive oil	60 ml	4 tbsp	4 tbsp
Mushrooms, sliced	175 g	6 oz	3 cups
White wine	200 ml	7 fl oz	scant 1 cup
Fillet steaks	4 x 175 g	4 x 6 oz	4 x ⅓ lb
Double (heavy) cream	150 ml	¼ pt	⅔ cup
Garlic clove, crushed	1	1	1
Chopped tarragon	30 ml	2 tbsp	2 tbsp
OR dried tarragon	10 ml	2 tsp	2 tsp
French mustard	10 ml	2 tsp	2 tsp
Salt and pepper			

TO GARNISH
Tarragon sprigs

TO SERVE
New potatoes and broccoli

1   Fry (sauté) the onions in half of the oil until softened. Add the mushrooms and cook for a further 2 minutes. Add the wine and simmer for 5 minutes.

2   Meanwhile, flatten the steaks with a rolling pin and fry in another pan in the remaining oil for 4–12 minutes.

3   Stir the cream, garlic, tarragon and mustard into the mixture and heat gently for 4–5 minutes. Season.

4   Serve the steaks on top of the sauce. Garnish with tarragon and serve with new potatoes and broccoli.

PREPARATION TIME: 10 MINUTES

COOKING TIME: 17 MINUTES

Alpine Beef Stroganoff

SERVES 6	METRIC	IMPERIAL	AMERICAN
Fillet OR rump steak	750 g	1½ lb	1½ lb
Unsalted (sweet) butter	50 g	2 oz	¼ cup
Onion, finely chopped	1	1	1
Mushrooms, finely sliced	100 g	4 oz	2 cups
Tomato purée (paste)	10 ml	2 tsp	2 tsp
French mustard	10 ml	2 tsp	2 tsp
Plain (all-purpose) flour	20 ml	4 tsp	4 tsp
Soured (dairy sour) cream	150 ml	¼ pt	⅔ cup
Salt and pepper			
Lemon juice to taste			
TO SERVE			
Boiled rice and salad			

1   Beat the steak flat between cling film (plastic wrap) or greaseproof (waxed) paper with a rolling pin. Cut into narrow short strips.

2   Heat half the butter and fry (sauté) the onion and mushrooms gently until soft and lightly golden.

3   Stir in the tomato purée, mustard and enough flour to absorb the fat. Cook over a very low heat for 2–3 minutes, then blend in the cream.

4   In another pan, fry the meat in the remaining butter until browned. Add to the sauce, season with salt, pepper and lemon juice. Serve with rice and salad.

PREPARATION TIME: 10 MINUTES
COOKING TIME: 10 MINUTES

Carbonnades à la Flamande

*T*he sweet taste of the casserole compliments the garlic crust surprisingly well. As with lots of casseroles, the flavour develops if you let it go cold and then reheat it later. Add the garlic crust at the end of the reheating stage and always make sure it is piping hot before serving.

SERVES 6	METRIC	IMPERIAL	AMERICAN
Lean braising steak, cut into neat, wide strips	1.5 kg	3 lb	3 lb
Unsalted (sweet) butter OR dripping	100 g	4 oz	½ cup
Olive oil	15 ml	1 tbsp	1 tbsp
Large onions, sliced	3	3	3
Garlic cloves, crushed	4	4	4
Salt and pepper			
Plain (all-purpose) flour	30 ml	2 tbsp	2 tbsp
Soft brown sugar	15 ml	1 tbsp	1 tbsp
Strong beef stock	300 ml	½ pt	1¼ cups
Brown ale	450 ml	¾ pt	2 cups
Red wine vinegar	15 ml	1 tbsp	1 tbsp
Bouquet garni	1	1	1
Bay leaves	2	2	2
GARLIC CRUST			
Unsalted (sweet) butter	225 g	8 oz	1 cup
Garlic cloves	3	3	3
French stick	1	1	1
TO SERVE			
Cauliflower with Almonds and Turkish Fried Carrots (see pages 140 and 125)			

1 Brown the beef quickly in the butter and oil and put aside.

2   Cook the onions until golden and add the garlic. Layer onions and beef in a deep casserole dish (Dutch oven) beginning with the onions. Lightly season the layers.

3   To the pan juices, add the flour and sugar and cook for 1 minute, stirring. Stir in a little of the stock until the mixture is smooth. Bring to the boil and add the remaining stock, ale and vinegar. Bring the mixture to the boil again. Put the bouquet garni and bay leaves into the casserole, pour the sauce over the meat and cook for 2½ hours in the oven at 160°C/325°F/gas mark 3.

4   For the garlic crust, melt the butter in a frying pan (skillet), add the garlic. Slice the bread into 2.5 cm/1 in thick slices and soak in the garlic butter.

5   Put the bread on top of the casserole, buttered side up. Cook for a further 15 minutes uncovered until the garlic crust is golden.

6   Serve with Cauliflower with Almonds and Turkish Fried Carrots.

PREPARATION TIME: 10 MINUTES
COOKING TIME: 3 HOURS

Stifado

*T*his is a Greek recipe and can be varied by using rabbit instead of beef. Stick to the feta cheese if you can (it freezes well), if not use a crumbly cheese like Cheshire or Wensleydale.

SERVES 6	METRIC	IMPERIAL	AMERICAN
Lean braising steak or shin beef, cut into cubes	1 kg	2¼ lb	2¼ lb
Seasoned flour	50 g	2 oz	½ cup
Oil	75 ml	5 tbsp	5 tbsp
Cumin seeds	1.5 ml	¼ tsp	¼ tsp
Piece cinnamon stick	5 cm	2 in	2 in
Tomato purée (paste)	45 ml	3 tbsp	3 tbsp
Herb vinegar	30 ml	2 tbsp	2 tbsp
Salt and pepper			
Beef stock	900 ml	1½ pts	3¾ cups
Sprigs of thyme	2	2	2
Small onions, peeled	450 g	1 lb	1 lb
Feta cheese, cubed	100 g	4 oz	1 cup

TO GARNISH			
Sprigs of thyme			

TO SERVE			
Rice, pitta bread and salad			

1   Toss the meat in seasoned flour, fry (sauté) in the oil and transfer to a casserole (Dutch oven).

2   Add the cumin, cinnamon stick and tomato purée to the remaining juices. Stir in the vinegar, salt and pepper, stock and thyme. Bring to the boil and pour over the meat.

3   Cover and cook in the over for 2½ hours at 160°C/ 325°F/gas mark 3 or a slow cooker for about 6 hours.

4   Plunge the onions into boiling water, drain and add to the casserole and cook for a further 30 minutes. Add the cubed cheese and return to the oven until the cheese begins to melt. Garnish with thyme. Serve with rice, pitta bread and salad.

PREPARATION TIME: 15 MINUTES

COOKING TIME: 3 HOURS

Peppered Steak

I know that classic peppered steak should be prepared with crushed black peppercorns, but I find mild green peppercorns give a much more pleasing flavour.

SERVES 4	METRIC	IMPERIAL	AMERICAN
Green peppercorns, crushed	60 ml	4 tbsp	4 tbsp
Fillet OR entrecôte steaks	4	4	4
Unsalted (sweet) butter	50 g	2 oz	¼ cup
Olive oil	15 ml	1 tbsp	1 tbsp
Brandy	30 ml	2 tbsp	2 tbsp
Double (heavy) cream	150 ml	¼ pt	⅔ cup
Salt			

TO SERVE
Buttered new potatoes and a green salad

1 Press the peppercorns into both sides of the steaks. Cook them in the butter and oil for 2 minutes (turning once) over a high heat. Lower the heat and cook for 5 minutes for rare, 8–9 minutes for medium rare and 12 minutes for well done steaks. Lift out the steaks and keep warm on a serving dish.

2 Add the brandy to the juices in the pan and set alight. Shake the pan and when the flames die down, stir in the cream, season with salt and pour over the steaks.

3 Serve with buttered new potatoes and a green salad.

PREPARATION TIME: 5 MINUTES
COOKING TIME: 8–15 MINUTES

Italian Lamb

SERVES 4	METRIC	IMPERIAL	AMERICAN
Lamb fillet, cut into medallions 5 mm/¼ in thick	750 g	1½ lb	1½ lb
Seasoned flour	30 ml	2 tbsp	2 tbsp
Olive oil	45 ml	3 tbsp	3 tbsp
Butter	25 g	1 oz	2 tbsp
Garlic clove, crushed	1	1	1
Button mushrooms, sliced	100 g	4 oz	2 cups
Parma ham, cut into thin strips	75 g	3 oz	¾ cup
Pesto (see page 157)	10 ml	2 tsp	2 tsp
Grated Parmesan cheese	45 ml	3 tbsp	3 tbsp

TO SERVE

Pasta with Vegetable Ribbons (see page 140) and a green salad

1 Flatten the lamb medallions slightly with a meat mallet or rolling pin and dust with the seasoned flour.

2 Quickly fry (sauté) in half the oil and butter, turning once. Remove the lamb and keep warm.

3 Using the remaining oil and butter, fry the garlic and mushrooms for 3 minutes, then add the ham and pesto and cook for a further minute.

4 Return the lamb to the pan and, stirring everything together, cook for a further 2 minutes.

5 Sprinkle with the Parmesan and serve with Pasta and Vegetable Ribbons and a green salad.

PREPARATION TIME: 10 MINUTES

COOKING TIME: 10 MINUTES

Rosemary Roasted Lamb Fillets

SERVES 6	METRIC	IMPERIAL	AMERICAN
Fillets of lamb	3 × 275 g	3 × 10 oz	3 × ⅔ lb
Large sprigs of fresh rosemary	2	2	2
Olive oil	45 ml	3 tbsp	3 tbsp
Garlic cloves, peeled but not crushed	8–10	8–10	8–10

TO GARNISH
Sprigs of rosemary

TO SERVE
Leek and Honey Sauce, Baked Fennel and Tomatoes (see pages 156 and 152) and roast potatoes

1   Cut any big pieces of fat off the lamb and reserve. Strip the leaves from the rosemary sprigs and put with the lamb, oil and garlic in a dish. Marinate overnight.

2   Melt the reserved lamb fat in a frying pan (skillet). Fry (sauté) the garlic and seal the lamb fillets on all sides. Place the garlic and fillets in a roasting tin (pan) and pour the marinade over. Roast at 200°C/400°F/gas mark 6 for 15 minutes (rare), 20 minutes (medium) or 25 minutes (well done).

3   Carve into thick slices, garnish with rosemary and surround with the roasted garlic cloves. Serve with Leek and Honey Sauce, Baked Fennel and Tomatoes and roast potatoes.

PREPARATION TIME: 5 MINUTES PLUS MARINATING TIME

COOKING TIME: 20–25 MINUTES

Lamb Medallions with Cognac

*T*hese tender lamb medallions take hardly any time at all to cook and the sauce adds a touch of elegance.

SERVES 4	METRIC	IMPERIAL	AMERICAN
Lamb fillet, cut into medallions 5 mm/¼ in thick	750 g	1½ lb	1½ lb
Black peppercorns, crushed	30 ml	2 tbsp	2 tbsp
Salt	1.5 ml	¼ tsp	¼ tsp
Garlic cloves, crushed	2	2	2
Unsalted (sweet) butter	50 g	2 oz	¼ cup
Cognac	60 ml	4 tbsp	4 tbsp

TO SERVE
Antibes Potatoes and French Beans with Feta and Sun-dried Tomatoes (see pages 133 and 150)

1 Flatten the lamb medallions slightly with a mallet or a rolling pin, coat with the crushed peppercorns and season with the salt.

2 Quickly fry (sauté) them with the garlic in the butter.

3 Add the cognac to the pan and set alight. Shake the pan until the flames have died down. Serve with the sauce poured over, with Antibes Potatoes and French Beans with Feta and Sun-dried Tomatoes.

PREPARATION TIME: 10 MINUTES

COOKING TIME: 10 MINUTES

Roasted Soy Lamb Fillets

*A*lthough the cooking time is short, you must set aside time in advance for marinating. Boned loin makes a delicious, but expensive, alternative to the neck fillets.

SERVES 4	METRIC	IMPERIAL	AMERICAN
Lamb neck fillets	2 × 350 g	2 × 12 oz	2 × ¾ lb

MARINADE			
Juice of 1 lime			
Soy sauce	30 ml	2 tbsp	2 tbsp
Olive oil	15 ml	1 tbsp	1 tbsp
Garlic clove, crushed	1	1	1

TO SERVE			
Orange Glazed Turnips and Galettes (see pages 142 and 134)			

1 Trim the lamb of fat and sinews. Mix the marinade ingredients together and pour over the lamb. Leave to marinate for at least 12 hours.

2 Remove the lamb from its marinade and roast on a rack in the oven at 230°C/450°F/gas mark 8 for 20 minutes (medium) or 25 minutes (well done).

3 Leave to rest for about 5 minutes before cutting into thin slices. Serve with Orange Glazed Turnips and Galettes.

PREPARATION TIME: 5 MINUTES PLUS MARINATING TIME
COOKING TIME: 20–25 MINUTES

Lamb Chops in Port

*Y*ou can cook this in a slow cooker for 5 hours if preferred – the perfect solution if you are having a busy day.

SERVES 4	METRIC	IMPERIAL	AMERICAN
Lamb loin chops	8	8	8
OR chump chops	4	4	4
Button mushrooms, quartered	100 g	4 oz	2 cups
Olive oil	15 ml	1 tbsp	1 tbsp
Onion, finely chopped	1	1	1
Port	150 ml	¼ pt	⅔ cup
Chicken stock	150 ml	¼ pt	⅔ cup
Redcurrant jelly (clear conserve)	30 ml	2 tbsp	2 tbsp
Salt and pepper			

TO SERVE
Jacket baked potatoes, courgettes (zucchini) and carrots

1   Fry (sauté) the chops and mushrooms in the oil in a flameproof casserole (Dutch oven) until golden brown. Set aside.

2   Fry the onions gently, stir in the port, stock, redcurrant jelly and seasoning. Boil for 2–3 minutes until the liquid reduces slightly and thickens. Return the chops.

3   Cover and cook in the oven for 1¼ hours at 175°C/ 350°F/gas mark 4 or on the hob gently for 45 minutes.

4   Serve with jacket baked potatoes, courgettes and carrots.

PREPARATION TIME: 10 MINUTES
COOKING TIME: 45 MINUTES (HOB) OR 1¼ HOURS (OVEN)

Tagine Barrogog Bis Basela

*W*hat? Yes, you did read it right! It's lamb stew, but oh so rich. The honey's sweetness is countered by the black pepper and spices.

SERVES 8	METRIC	IMPERIAL	AMERICAN
Boned shoulder, leg or neck fillet of lamb, cut into large pieces	1 kg	2¼ lb	2¼ lb
Salt			
Black pepper	10 ml	2 tsp	2 tsp
Saffron powder OR turmeric	2.5 ml	½ tsp	½ tsp
Ground ginger	5 ml	1 tsp	1 tsp
Garlic cloves, crushed	2	2	2
Large onion, grated	1	1	1
Small bunch of parsley, finely chopped	1	1	1
Oil	60 ml	4 tbsp	4 tbsp
Prunes, stoned (pitted) and chopped	450 g	1 lb	2⅔ cups
Cinnamon	10 ml	2 tsp	2 tsp
Honey	15–60 ml	1–4 tbsp	1–4 tbsp
Orange flower water	45 ml	3 tbsp	3 tbsp
TO GARNISH			
Blanched almonds, chopped			
TO SERVE			
Tomato salad and French bread			

1   Put the lamb in a saucepan with a little salt, the pepper, saffron, ginger, garlic, onion, parsley and 45 ml/3 tbsp of the oil. Add enough water to cover and simmer, covered, for 1½ hours or until the meat is very tender.

2 Add the prunes and cinnamon and cook for a further 15 minutes.

3 Add the honey and the orange water and cook for a few more minutes until the sauce is quite thick.

4 Just before serving, fry (sauté) the almonds in the remaining oil and sprinkle over the meat. Serve with a tomato salad and French bread.

PREPARATION TIME: 10 MINUTES
COOKING TIME: 1 HOUR 50 MINUTES

Leg of Lamb in Red Wine

*A*nother delectable variation on a simple roast which won't spoil once cooked, while you enjoy time with your guests.

SERVES ABOUT 8	METRIC	IMPERIAL	AMERICAN
Leg of lamb	2 kg	4½ lb	4½ lb
Garlic cloves, cut into slivers	2	2	2
A few small sprigs of rosemary			
Oil	15 ml	1 tbsp	1 tbsp
Salt and pepper			
Ground ginger	10 ml	2 tsp	2 tsp
Unsalted (sweet) butter	50 g	2 oz	¼ cup
Onions, sliced	2	2	2
Carrots, chopped	2	2	2
Sprigs of thyme	4	4	4
Red wine	300 ml	½ pt	1¼ cups
Redcurrant jelly (clear conserve)	30 ml	2 tbsp	2 tbsp
TO SERVE			
Creamy Courgette Bake (see page 127), roast potatoes and carrots			

1   Stab the lamb with the point of a sharp knife and push garlic slivers and rosemary into these holes.

2   Rub the skin with the oil, a little salt and pepper and the ginger.

3   Melt the butter in a roasting tin (pan) and quickly brown the lamb all over. Remove from the tin and fry (sauté) the onions and carrots until golden brown. Put the sprigs of thyme on top of the vegetables and the meat on top. Cover with foil. Roast at 220°C/425°F/gas mark 7 for 25 minutes.

Pour the wine over, reduce the heat to 180°C/350°F/gas mark 4 for a further 1¼ hours, basting 2–3 times.

4 Remove the joint, strain the cooking juices and add the redcurrant jelly. Boil until reduced by a third. Remove any fat from the juices and season if necessary. Pour into a sauce boat and serve the lamb with Creamy Courgette Bake, roast potatoes and carrots.

PREPARATION TIME: 10 MINUTES

COOKING TIME: 2 HOURS

Braised Lamb with Herbes de Provence

*houlder of lamb is cheaper than leg and just as tasty. Choose a lean one and trim it well of fat. This dish is even better if left to get cold, then skimmed and reheated the following day.

SERVES 6–8	METRIC	IMPERIAL	AMERICAN
Olive oil	30 ml	2 tbsp	2 tbsp
Boned shoulder of lamb	1.5–1.75kg	3–4 lb	3–4 lb
Garlic cloves, halved	2	2	2
Large onion, quartered	1	1	1
Herbes de Provence	7.5 ml	1½ tsp	1½ tsp
Stock OR water	600 ml	1 pt	2½ cups
Dry wine, red OR white	60 ml	4 tbsp	4 tbsp
Large leeks, cut into short lengths	2	2	2
Carrots, cut into short lengths	450 g	1 lb	1 lb
Small potatoes, unpeeled	450 g	1 lb	1 lb

1 Heat the oil in a flameproof casserole (Dutch oven) and brown the meat on all sides. Add the garlic and onion with the herbs, stock or water and wine. Bring to the boil, cover and cook in the oven for 1 hour at 180°C/350°F/gas mark 4.

2 Add the leeks and carrots to the casserole and cook for a further 30 minutes. Add the potatoes and cook for another 30 minutes.

3 Skim the surface and serve.

PREPARATION TIME: 10 MINUTES	
COOKING TIME: 2 HOURS	

Pescada à la Marina

*T*his is one of my favourite ways of serving fish – popular with adults and children alike. Leftovers are good cold.

SERVES 6	METRIC	IMPERIAL	AMERICAN
Haddock OR cod fillets, cut into strips	750 g	1½ lb	1½ lb
Olive oil	60 ml	4 tbsp	4 tbsp
Lemon juice	30 ml	2 tbsp	2 tbsp
Small onion, finely chopped	1	1	1
Garlic clove, crushed	1	1	1
Bay leaves	2	2	2
Salt	5 ml	1 tsp	1 tsp
Black pepper			
A pinch of grated nutmeg			
Egg, lightly beaten	1	1	1
Fresh white breadcrumbs	100 g	4 oz	2 cups
Oil for frying			
TO SERVE			
Lemon Potatoes (see page 129) and salad			

1 Put the fish into a shallow dish. Blend the next 8 ingredients and pour over. Leave to marinate for at least 1 hour, turning from time to time.

2 Dry the fish on kitchen paper, dip in egg then breadcrumbs. Leave to harden before frying.

3 Fry (sauté) the fish on both sides in hot oil and drain on kitchen paper.

4 Serve the fish hot with Lemon Potatoes and salad.

PREPARATION TIME: 10 MINUTES PLUS MARINATING TIME

COOKING TIME: 6 MINUTES

Trout in Lemon Butter Sauce

*T*his works just as well with whole fish, but I prefer to use fillets as they're less fiddly to eat.

SERVES 4	METRIC	IMPERIAL	AMERICAN
Large trout fillets	4	4	4
Dried rosemary	2.5 ml	½ tsp	½ tsp
Salt	2.5 ml	½ tsp	½ tsp
Pepper	1.5 ml	¼ tsp	¼ tsp
Plain (all-purpose) flour	25 g	1 oz	¼ cup
Sunflower oil	120 ml	4 fl oz	½ cup
Butter	50 g	2 oz	¼ cup
Juice of 1 lemon			
Finely chopped parsley	30 ml	2 tbsp	2 tbsp

TO SERVE
Boiled potatoes, Garlicky French Beans (see page 144) and sweetcorn (corn)

1   Sprinkle the fish with the rosemary, salt and pepper and coat with flour.

2   Fry (sauté) the fish in the oil until just cooked (4–5 minutes). Remove the fish and keep warm.

3   Pour off the oil, add the butter, lemon juice and parsley and cook for about 1 minute, stirring any residue from the bottom of the pan. Pour the sauce over the fish.

4   Serve with boiled potatoes, Garlicky French Beans and sweetcorn.

PREPARATION TIME: 5 MINUTES

COOKING TIME: 6 MINUTES

Trout in Pernod Sauce

*D*on't be tempted to add more Pernod than suggested. This sauce just needs a hint of it to match the mushrooms and cream. More pernod would kill the trout's delicate flavour and destroy the balance of the sauce.

SERVES 4	METRIC	IMPERIAL	AMERICAN
Large fillets of trout	4	4	4
Seasoned flour for coating			
Unsalted (sweet) butter	100 g	4 oz	½ cup
Button mushrooms, thinly sliced	225 g	8 oz	4 cups
Garlic clove, crushed	1	1	1
Pernod OR Pastis	45 ml	3 tbsp	3 tbsp
Double (heavy) cream	150 ml	¼ pt	⅔ cup
Salt and black pepper			
TO SERVE			
Boiled or baked potatoes and salad			

1   Coat the trout fillets in seasoned flour and fry (sauté) in the butter for 4–5 minutes. Transfer to a serving dish and keep warm.

2   Fry the mushrooms and garlic in the trout juices over a gentle heat for 3–4 minutes.

3   Stir in the Pernod or Pastis and simmer for 3–4 minutes.

4   Add the cream and seasoning and heat gently. Pour the sauce over the trout and serve with boiled or baked potatoes and salad.

PREPARATION TIME: 5 MINUTES

COOKING TIME: 10 MINUTES

Salmon Casserole

*T*his simple but tasty casserole is made with mostly store cupboard ingredients – ideal for impromptu guests.

SERVES 4	METRIC	IMPERIAL	AMERICAN
Unsalted (sweet) butter	25 g	1 oz	2 tbsp
Plain (all-purpose) flour	25 g	1 oz	¼ cup
Fish stock	300 ml	½ pt	1¼ cups
White wine	300 ml	½ pt	1¼ cups
Single (light) cream	300 ml	½ pt	1¼ cups
New potatoes, boiled	750 g	1½ lb	1½ lb
Can pink salmon, drained	396 g	14 oz	1 large
Salt and pepper			
Bunch of watercress	1	1	1

TO SERVE
Baby carrots and peas

1   Melt the butter, then add the flour and cook for 1 minute, stirring all the time. Remove from the heat and gradually stir in the fish stock, then the wine and return to the heat. Bring to the boil and cook, stirring, until thickened. Reduce the heat and stir in the cream.

2   Add the potatoes and salmon, discarding any skin and bone. Season well.

3   Cook for about 3 minutes to heat all the ingredients. Chop the watercress, reserving a few sprigs for garnish, and fold the chopped watercress into the fish mixture, being careful not to break up the salmon too much.

4   Garnish with the reserved sprigs of watercress. Serve with baby carrots and peas.

PREPARATION TIME: 15 MINUTES
COOKING TIME: 6 MINUTES

Sole Knots

*T*ying the sole strips into knots is a bit fiddly, but worth the effort because the finished dish looks so attractive. However, if you haven't got time, simply cut the fish into pieces.

SERVES 6	METRIC	IMPERIAL	AMERICAN
Sole fillets, skinned and cut into 6 long strips	900 g	2 lb	2 lb
Onion, finely chopped	1	1	1
Butter	50 g	2 oz	¼ cup
Tomatoes, skinned, seeded and chopped	6	6	6
Anchovy fillets, chopped	6	6	6
Button mushrooms, sliced	175 g	6 oz	3 cups
Salt and pepper			

TO GARNISH
Croûtons

TO SERVE
Broccoli, sweetcorn and buttered new potatoes

1 Tie the strips of fish into knots and put into an ovenproof dish.

2 Fry (sauté) the onion in the butter and when golden add the tomatoes and cook together for 2–3 minutes.

3 Add the anchovy fillets, mushrooms, salt and pepper and cook for 2 minutes. Spoon this mixture over the sole knots.

4 Cover and bake in the oven at 190°C/375°F/gas mark 5 for 25 minutes. Garnish with croûtons and serve with broccoli, sweetcorn and buttered new potatoes.

PREPARATION TIME: 15 MINUTES
COOKING TIME: 30 MINUTES

Heavenly Fish Dish

*T*his recipe is a cross between a pie and a casserole and the ratio of prawns (shrimp) to cod gives it a really up-market taste and appearance.

SERVES 6	METRIC	IMPERIAL	AMERICAN
Cod steaks	6 × 100 g	6 × 4 oz	6 × ¼ lb
Milk	450 ml	¾ pt	2 cups
Peppercorns	6	6	6
Bay leaves	2	2	2
Leeks, thinly sliced	2	2	2
Unsalted (sweet) butter	50 g	2 oz	¼ cup
Plain (all-purpose) flour	25 g	1 oz	¼ cup
White wine	250 ml	8 fl oz	1 cup
Dried dill (dill weed)	10 ml	2 tsp	2 tsp
Dill seed	5 ml	1 tsp	1 tsp
Lemon juice	25 ml	1½ tbsp	1½ tbsp
Salt and pepper			
Peeled prawns (shrimp)	450 g	1 lb	4 cups
Tomatoes, chopped	4	4	4
Potatoes, cooked and thinly sliced	750 g	1½ lb	1½ lb
Olive oil	30 ml	2 tbsp	2 tbsp
Grated Parmesan cheese	30 ml	2 tbsp	2 tbsp
TO SERVE			
Roasted vegetables and a green salad			

1 Put the cod, milk, peppercorns and bay leaves into a saucepan. Bring to the boil, then simmer for 6–7 minutes.

2 Remove the fish and break into biggish flakes before putting into an ovenproof dish. Strain the milk and set aside.

3 Fry (sauté) the leeks gently in the butter for 5 minutes. Stir in the flour and cook for 1 minute. Gradually stir in the reserved milk and the wine and cook, stirring all the time, until thickened and smooth.

4 Remove from the heat and add the dill and dill seed, lemon juice and salt and pepper.

5 Arrange the prawns and tomatoes on top of the cod and pour the sauce over. Top with the sliced potatoes, brush them with olive oil and sprinkle with the Parmesan.

6 Cook in the oven at 190°C/375°F/gas mark 5 for about 30 minutes until the topping is golden brown. Serve with any colourful roasted vegetables and a crisp green salad.

PREPARATION TIME: 20 MINUTES

COOKING TIME: 45 MINUTES

Seafood Surprises

*T*hese individual seafood parcels take quite a bit of space in the oven – something to think about when deciding what vegetables to serve with them.

SERVES 4	METRIC	IMPERIAL	AMERICAN
Leeks, thinly sliced	4	4	4
Cod fillets	4 x 100 g	4 x 4 oz	4 x ¼ lb
Peeled prawns (shrimp)	100 g	4 oz	1 cup
Dill (dill weed), roughly chopped	30 ml	2 tbsp	2 tbsp
Salt and pepper			
Unsalted (sweet) butter, melted	25 g	1 oz	2 tbsp
Juice of 1 lemon			

TO GARNISH
Lemon slices

TO SERVE
Boiled rice and Carrots with Orange and Cardamom (see page 141)

1   Cut 4 circles of baking parchment, about 30 cm/12 in diameter. Fold in half, then open out again.

2   Scatter the leeks over half of each circle and top with the cod. Divide the prawns equally between the parcels, sprinkle over the dill and seasoning and pour on the melted butter and lemon juice.

3   Fold over the empty half of each parcel and roll the edges tightly together. Place on a baking sheet and cook in the oven at 200°C/400°F/gas mark 6 for 10–15 minutes.

4   Put each parcel on a dinner plate and garnish with the lemon. Serve at once, opening at the table. Serve with boiled rice and Carrots with Orange and Cardamom.

PREPARATION TIME: 15 MINUTES

COOKING TIME: 10–15 MINUTES

Thai Grilled Fish

*T*his is a light and delicious way of serving any thin white fish fillets – and so simple to prepare.

SERVES 4	METRIC	IMPERIAL	AMERICAN
Plaice fillets, skinned	4	4	4
Salt	5 ml	1 tsp	1 tsp
Juice of 2 limes			
Soft brown sugar	90 ml	6 tbsp	6 tbsp

TO SERVE
Zingy Carrots with Courgettes (see page 136) and rice

1   Sprinkle the fillets with the salt and lime juice and leave to marinate for 20–25 minutes.

2   Sprinkle the sugar over and grill (broil) for about 5 minutes until the fillets are cooked and the sugar has caramelised.

3   Serve with Zingy Carrots and Courgettes and rice.

PREPARATION TIME: 5 MINUTES PLUS MARINATING TIME

COOKING TIME: 5 MINUTES

Marinated Salmon Steaks

*H*ere is another recipe that takes minimal cooking time, although you must set aside time for marinating. I love the taste of salmon and this marinade makes it even better and intriguingly different.

SERVES 6	METRIC	IMPERIAL	AMERICAN
Vegetable oil	100 ml	4 fl oz	½ cup
Juice and grated rind of 2 limes			
Orange juice	45 ml	3 tbsp	3 tbsp
Clear honey	5 ml	1 tsp	1 tsp
Green cardamoms, crushed	2	2	2
Salmon steaks	6 × 175 g	6 × 6 oz	6 × ⅓ lb

TO SERVE
New potatoes in Anchovy Cream (see page 155) and a mixed salad

1   Mix together 75 ml/5 tbsp of the oil with the lime rind and juice, the orange juice, honey and the cardamom seeds. Pour this marinade over the fish and leave for 12 hours if possible.

2   Drain, reserving the marinade. Grill (broil) the salmon for about 4 minutes on each side.

3   Meanwhile bring the marinade to the boil and keep warm. Serve the steaks with the sauce poured over, accompanied by new potatoes in Anchovy Cream and a mixed salad.

PREPARATION TIME: 5 MINUTES PLUS MARINATING TIME
COOKING TIME: 10 MINUTES

Fish Parcels

*W*eaving the bacon to make the wrapping for the fish is a little bit fiddly, but after the first one it's plain sailing! The little parcels hold together well during cooking and they look and taste delightful.

SERVES 4	METRIC	IMPERIAL	AMERICAN
Rashers (slices) streaky bacon, rinded	24	24	24
Cod fillets	4 × 100 g	4 × 4 oz	4 × ¼ lb
Onion, finely chopped	1	1	1
Unsalted (sweet) butter	50 g	2 oz	¼ cup
White wine	150 ml	¼ pt	⅔ cup
Dried tarragon	2.5 ml	½ tsp	½ tsp
Double (heavy) cream	60 ml	4 tbsp	4 tbsp

TO SERVE
Baked potatoes and Garlicky French Beans (see page 144)

1   Stretch the bacon rashers with the back of a knife.

2   Weave 6 of them into a square and put one of the fish portions into the centre. Fold the overlapping bacon around the fish to enclose it. Repeat with the remaining bacon and fish to make another 3 parcels.

3   Fry (sauté) the onion in the butter until soft, then add the fish parcels and fry for 3 minutes until slightly browned. Add the wine and tarragon to the pan, bring to the boil, cover and simmer for 10 minutes. Add the cream and seasoning to taste. Heat through and serve with baked potatoes and Garlicky French Beans.

PREPARATION TIME: 20 MINUTES
COOKING TIME: 13–14 MINUTES

Vegetarian Main Courses

*N*one of the following recipes contains meat or fish. If, however, you are cooking for serious vegetarians, make sure that any cheese or condiments you use are suitable (even Worcestershire sauce has anchovies in it) – check the labels before you buy. And don't be afraid to 'go meatless' for a change – all the dishes in this chapter would tempt even the most hardened carnivore!

Sensational Onion Tart

*O*nion tart sounds a bit plain, doesn't it? But this one is rich, creamy and very satisfying.

SERVES 6	METRIC	IMPERIAL	AMERICAN
Shortcrust pastry (basic pie crust)	225 g	8 oz	½ lb
Large onions, finely sliced	3	3	3
Butter	25 g	1 oz	2 tbsp
Egg	1	1	1
Egg yolk	1	1	1
Double (heavy) cream	150 ml	¼ pt	⅔ cup
Salt and pepper			
Grated nutmeg	2.5 ml	½ tsp	½ tsp

TO SERVE
Sugar Browned Potatoes and Zingy Carrots and Courgettes (see pages 130 and 136)

1   Line a flan (pie) ring set on a baking sheet with the pastry and chill while preparing the filling.

2   Fry (sauté) the onions in the butter until soft.

3   Beat the egg, egg yolk and cream together and stir into the onions. Season with salt, pepper and nutmeg.

4   Pour into the flan ring and bake at 200°C/400°F/gas mark 6 for 30 minutes until golden and bubbling. Serve with Sugar Browned Potatoes and Zingy Carrots and Courgettes.

PREPARATION TIME: 10 MINUTES
COOKING TIME: 35 MINUTES

Pizza Puffs

*T*he flaky pastry bases on these mini pizzas are a pleasant change from the traditional ones.

SERVES 6	METRIC	IMPERIAL	AMERICAN
Sheets ready-rolled flaky pastry	3 × 20 cm	3 × 8 in	3 × 8 in
Spring onions (scallions), chopped	3	3	3
Butter, melted	25 g	1 oz	2 tbsp
Rind and juice of 1 lemon			
Salt and pepper			
Pesto (see page 157)	30 ml	2 tbsp	2 tbsp
Tomatoes, sliced	350 g	12 oz	¾ lb
Courgettes (zucchini), cut into thin slices	225 g	8 oz	2 cups
TO GARNISH			
Grated Parmesan cheese			
TO SERVE			
Mixed salad			

1 From the pastry cut out 6 rounds, 11 cm/4½ in diameter. Prick the circles with a fork and bake at 230°C/450°F/gas mark 8 for about 8 minutes until risen and golden.

2 Meanwhile, stir the onions into the melted butter with the lemon rind and the lemon juice and season well.

3 Spread each cooked pastry circle with pesto and arrange the slices of tomato and courgette alternately. Brush with the melted butter mixture.

4 Return to the oven and cook for 12–14 minutes or until the courgettes are softened and the edges of the pastry are puffed and golden. Sprinkle with Parmesan and serve hot with a mixed salad.

PREPARATION TIME: 10 MINUTES

COOKING TIME: 20–24 MINUTES

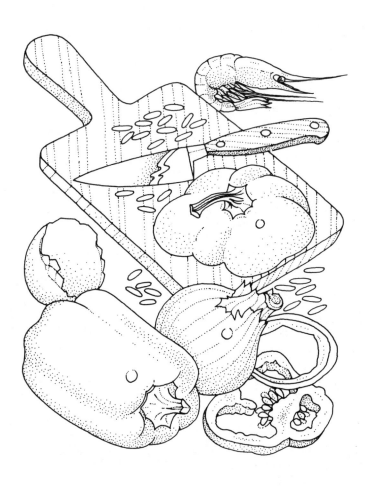

Broccoli and Roquefort Tagliatelle

*T*o make this dish a little more substantial, sprinkle fresh breadcrumbs and grated cheese over the top and put under the grill (broiler) for 5 minutes before serving.

SERVES 4	METRIC	IMPERIAL	AMERICAN
Double (heavy) cream	150 ml	¼ pt	⅔ cup
Roquefort cheese, crumbled	100 g	4 oz	¼ lb
Broccoli florets, cooked until just tender	225 g	8 oz	½ lb
Salt and pepper			
Tagliatelle, cooked	225 g	8 oz	½ lb

TO GARNISH
Chopped parsley and toasted flaked almonds

TO SERVE
Tomato salad and crunchy French bread

1   Put the cream into a saucepan and add the cheese. Heat gently, stirring, until the cheese melts.

2   Stir in the broccoli and seasoning.

3   Fold the tagliatelle through the sauce, heat through gently, and garnish with chopped parsley and a few toasted, flaked almonds. Serve with a tomato salad and crunchy French bread.

PREPARATION TIME: 15 MINUTES (INCLUDING COOKING BROCCOLI AND TAGLIATELLE)

COOKING TIME: 5 MINUTES

Red and White Aubergines

SERVES 4	METRIC	IMPERIAL	AMERICAN
Large aubergines (eggplants)	2	2	2
Salt			
Olive oil	45 ml	3 tbsp	3 tbsp
Red (bell) pepper, chopped	1	1	1
Shallots, chopped	3	3	3
Pepper			
Cherry tomatoes, halved	175 g	6 oz	⅓ lb
Firm goat's cheese, sliced	175 g	6 oz	⅓ lb
Chopped thyme	10 ml	2 tsp	2 tsp
TO SERVE			
Pasta and salad			

1   Halve the aubergines lengthways and sprinkle with salt. Leave for 30 minutes. Drain and dry on kitchen paper.

2   Place in a roasting tin (pan), brush with a little of the oil and bake at 200°C/400°F/gas mark 6 for 35–40 minutes. Scoop out the flesh to within 1 cm/½ in of the skin. Chop the flesh.

3   Fry (sauté) the red pepper and shallots in 15 ml/1 tbsp of the remaining oil until soft. Add the aubergine flesh and pepper and mix well.

4   Pile this mixture into the shells and arrange the tomatoes and goat's cheese in alternate rows along the top. Drizzle with the remaining oil and sprinkle with the thyme. Bake for 25 minutes. Serve with pasta and salad.

PREPARATION TIME: 20 MINUTES PLUS SALTING TIME

COOKING TIME: 60–65 MINUTES

Roast Vegetable Casserole

*T*his really is a hearty casserole and all you need with it is bread or garlic bread to mop up the sauce.

SERVES 6	METRIC	IMPERIAL	AMERICAN
Large aubergine (eggplant), cut into chunks	1	1	1
Salt			
Large onions, roughly chopped	2	2	2
Red AND green (bell) peppers, thickly sliced	2 each	2 each	2 each
Garlic cloves, crushed	3	3	3
Courgettes (zucchini), cut into chunks	450 g	1 lb	1 lb
Dried oregano	5 ml	1 tsp	1 tsp
Olive oil	90 ml	6 tbsp	6 tbsp
Potatoes, cut into chunks and boiled for 10 minutes	1.1 kg	2½ lb	2½ lb
Can chopped tomatoes	400 g	14 oz	1 large
Jar tomato sauce for pasta	400 g	14 oz	1 large
A few drops of Tabasco sauce			
French mustard	15 ml	1 tbsp	1 tbsp
Salt and pepper			
Mushrooms, chopped	450 g	1 lb	6 cups
Can sweetcorn (corn) OR baby corn cobs	400 g	14 oz	1 large
TO GARNISH			
Watercress			
TO SERVE			
Crusty bread			

1 Sprinkle the aubergine chunks with salt and leave to stand for 30 minutes. Drain, pat dry with kitchen paper and put them in a roasting dish with the onions, peppers, garlic and courgettes. Sprinkle with the oregano and most of the oil, tossing to ensure they are well coated.

2 In another dish, mix the potatoes with the tomatoes, remaining oil, tomato sauce, Tabasco, mustard and salt and pepper.

3 Cook both dishes in the oven at 190°C/375°F/gas mark 5 for 1 hour.

4 Add the mushrooms and corn to the mixed vegetables and cook for a further 30 minutes. Transfer the mixed vegetables to a warm serving dish and arrange the potato and tomato mixture around the outside. Garnish with sprigs of watercress and serve hot with crusty bread.

PREPARATION TIME: 20 MINUTES PLUS SALTING TIME

COOKING TIME: 1½ HOURS

Feta Cauliflower with Tomato Sauce

*T*he cinnamon and lemon juice give this dish quite an interesting middle-eastern flavour.

SERVES 4	METRIC	IMPERIAL	AMERICAN
Garlic cloves, crushed	3	3	3
Large onion, finely chopped	1	1	1
Olive oil	60 ml	4 tbsp	4 tbsp
Cans chopped tomatoes	2 × 400 g	2 × 14 oz	2 large
Bay leaf	1	1	1
Dried oregano	10 ml	2 tsp	2 tsp
Cinnamon stick	5 cm	2 in	2 in
Salt and pepper			
Large cauliflower, cut into florets and cooked until just tender	1	1	1
Lemon juice	15 ml	1 tbsp	1 tbsp
Feta cheese, crumbled	100 g	4 oz	1 cup
Emmental (Swiss) cheese, grated	100 g	4 oz	1 cup

TO SERVE			
Baked Sliced Potatoes (see page 135) and a green salad			

1   Cook the garlic and onion in half the oil until soft, then add the tomatoes, herbs, cinnamon stick and seasoning. Bring to the boil and simmer for 5 minutes.

2   Put the cauliflower into a shallow ovenproof dish and cover with the tomato sauce, discarding the cinnamon stick and bay leaf at this stage.

3   Sprinkle with the lemon juice and remaining oil and cover with the cheeses.

4   Bake in the oven at 190°C/375°F/gas mark 5 for 25 minutes. Serve immediately with Baked Sliced Potatoes and a green salad.

| PREPARATION TIME: 15 MINUTES |
| COOKING TIME: 35 MINUTES |

Potato Pesto Pie

SERVES 4	METRIC	IMPERIAL	AMERICAN
Onion, sliced	1	1	1
Butter	75 g	3 oz	⅓ cup
Garlic cloves, crushed	2	2	2
Pesto (see page 157)	30 ml	2 tbsp	2 tbsp
Potatoes, thinly sliced and boiled for 5 minutes	750 g	1½ lb	1½ lb
Puff pastry (paste)	175 g	6 oz	⅓ lb
Grated Parmesan cheese	75 g	3 oz	¾ cup
Salt and pepper			
Double (heavy) cream	120 ml	4 fl oz	½ cup
Egg (size 1), beaten	1	1	1
Extra beaten egg to glaze			

| TO SERVE |
| Baked Fennel and Tomatoes (see page 152) |

1   Fry (sauté) the onion in the butter for 5 minutes, then add the garlic and pesto and cook for a further minute. Layer in a pie dish with the potatoes, Parmesan and seasoning. Beat the cream and egg and pour over.

2   Top with the pastry and glaze with egg. Cut two slits in the pastry. Bake in the oven at 200°C/400°F/gas mark 6 for 1 hour. Serve with Baked Fennel and Tomatoes.

| PREPARATION TIME: 10 MINUTES |
| COOKING TIME: 1 HOUR 10 MINUTES |

Risotto Bake

$\mathcal{S}$erve this 'flan' cut into wedges. It is delicious when topped with extra crème fraîche and Parmesan, or a rich tomato sauce.

SERVES 8	METRIC	IMPERIAL	AMERICAN
Leeks, thinly sliced	450 g	1 lb	4 cups
Olive oil	15 ml	1 tbsp	1 tbsp
Butter	50 g	2 oz	¼ cup
Onion, finely chopped	1	1	1
Garlic clove, crushed	1	1	1
Risotto rice	225 g	8 oz	1 cup
White wine	150 ml	¼ pt	⅔ cup
Vegetable stock	450 ml	¾ pt	2 cups
Eggs, lightly beaten	2	2	2
Crème fraîche	50 g	2 oz	¼ cup
Chopped parsley	30 ml	2 tbsp	2 tbsp
Chopped sage	15 ml	1 tbsp	1 tbsp
Grated nutmeg	1.5 ml	¼ tsp	¼ tsp
Grated Parmesan cheese	50 g	2 oz	½ cup
Salt and pepper			

TO SERVE
Cauliflower Sautéed with Coriander and
    Buttered Carrots and Parsley (see pages 143 and 126)

1   Fry (sauté) the leeks in the oil for 10 minutes and set aside.

2   Using most of the butter, fry the onion and garlic for 3 minutes, stir in the rice and cook for 1 minute. When the rice is transparent, stir in the wine and simmer until it is absorbed.

3   Add the stock, little by little, and cook until this is absorbed (about 20–25 minutes). Add the rice to the leeks.

4   Mix together the eggs, crème fraîche, parsley, sage, nutmeg and most of the Parmesan. Stir this into the rice. Add seasoning and turn into a greased and lined flan dish (pie pan). Sprinkle with the remaining cheese and dot the remaining butter over the surface. Bake in the oven at 200°C/400°F/gas mark 6 for 25 minutes until set and golden brown. Serve with Cauliflower Sautéed with Coriander and Buttered Carrots with Parsley.

PREPARATION TIME: 10 MINUTES

COOKING TIME: 1 HOUR

Turkish Aubergines and Tomatoes

*T*hese aubergines and tomatoes can also be served as a spicy accompaniment to any grilled meat dish, in which case you would not need to make the topping.

SERVES 4	METRIC	IMPERIAL	AMERICAN
Aubergines (eggplants), chopped	800 g	1¾ lb	1¾ lb
Salt			
Olive oil	60 ml	4 tbsp	4 tbsp
Large onion, chopped	1	1	1
Large tomatoes, skinned and chopped	6	6	6
Garlic cloves, crushed	2	2	2
Chopped parsley	30 ml	2 tbsp	2 tbsp
Ground allspice	1.5 ml	¼ tsp	¼ tsp
Ground cinnamon	1.5 ml	¼ tsp	¼ tsp
Sugar	1.5 ml	¼ tsp	¼ tsp
Pepper			
Butter, for greasing			
TOPPING			
Feta cheese, crumbled	30 ml	2 tbsp	2 tbsp
Fresh breadcrumbs	45 ml	3 tbsp	3 tbsp
Butter	15 ml	1 tbsp	1 tbsp
TO SERVE			
Turkish Fried Carrots and Lemon Potatoes (see pages 125 and 129)			

1 Sprinkle the aubergines with salt and leave to stand for 30 minutes. Drain and dry on kitchen paper. Fry them in the oil until they start to go pale golden brown, then add the onions.

2 When these are soft, add the tomatoes, garlic, parsley, spices, sugar and pepper. Stirring occasionally, simmer for 5 minutes.

3 Transfer the mixture to a buttered ovenproof dish. Top with the cheese and breadcrumbs and dot with butter. Bake in the oven at 190°C/375°F/gas mark 5 for 30 minutes. Serve with Turkish Fried Carrots and Lemon Potatoes.

PREPARATION TIME: 10 MINUTES PLUS SALTING TIME

COOKING TIME: 45 MINUTES

Leek and Goat's Cheese Pie

*T*his pie is also good with pasta and tomato sauce as a warm and filling supper dish.

SERVES 8	METRIC	IMPERIAL	AMERICAN
Shortcrust pastry (basic pie crust)	225 g	8 oz	½ lb
Leeks, sliced	900 g	2 lb	2 lb
Butter	50 g	2 oz	¼ cup
Oil	15 ml	1 tbsp	1 tbsp
Goat's cheese, crumbled	100 g	4 oz	1 cup
Double (heavy) cream	300 ml	½ pt	1¼ cups
Eggs (size 1), lightly beaten	2	2	2
Salt and pepper			
Flaky pastry (paste)	225 g	8 oz	½ lb
Beaten egg to glaze			

TO SERVE
Tomato salad

1   Roll out the shortcrust pastry to line the base of a 23 cm/9 in pie dish.

2   Fry (sauté) the leeks in the butter and oil for 5 minutes. Spoon into the pie dish. Top with the cheese.

3   Beat the cream and eggs together and pour this mixture into the pie dish and season.

4   Roll out the puff pastry and top the pie with it. Glaze with beaten egg, then bake in the oven at 200°C/400°F/gas mark 6 for 40 minutes until the pie is golden. Serve warm with a tomato salad.

PREPARATION TIME: 15 MINUTES
COOKING TIME: 45 MINUTES

Rich Tomato and Aubergine Casserole

*T*his dish makes a satisfying meal in its own right, but it is also good served as an accompaniment to plain grilled meats.

SERVES 4	METRIC	IMPERIAL	AMERICAN
Onion, chopped	1	1	1
Cumin seeds	5 ml	1 tsp	1 tsp
Ground ginger	15 ml	1 tbsp	1 tbsp
Olive oil	45 ml	3 tbsp	3 tbsp
Large aubergines (eggplants), cut in small cubes	2	2	2
Red wine	300 ml	½ pt	1¼ cups
Can chopped tomatoes	400 g	14 oz	1 large
Sun-dried tomatoes (preserved in oil), chopped	45 ml	3 tbsp	3 tbsp
Tomato purée (paste)	30 ml	2 tbsp	2 tbsp
Sugar	10 ml	2 tsp	2 tsp

TO SERVE
Garlic bread and a crisp green salad

1   Fry (sauté) the onion, cumin seeds and ginger in the oil until the onion has softened.

2   Add the aubergines and cook for 5 minutes, stirring.

3   Pour in the wine, then the tomatoes, sun-dried tomatoes, tomato purée and sugar. Simmer for 30 minutes until the aubergines are tender. Serve with lots of garlic bread and a crisp green salad.

PREPARATION TIME: 10 MINUTES
COOKING TIME: 40 MINUTES

Chilli Non Carne

SERVES 4	METRIC	IMPERIAL	AMERICAN
Onion, chopped	1	1	1
Olive oil	45 ml	3 tbsp	3 tbsp
Large green (bell) pepper, chopped	1	1	1
Carrots, sliced	2	2	2
Garlic clove, crushed	1	1	1
Cumin seeds, crushed	5 ml	1 tsp	1 tsp
Chilli powder	5–10 ml	1–2 tsp	1–2 tsp
Celery sticks, sliced	2	2	2
Courgettes (zucchini), sliced	4	4	4
Can tomatoes	400 g	14 oz	1 large
Tomato purée (paste)	15 ml	1 tbsp	1 tbsp
Vegetable stock	150 ml	¼ pt	⅔ cup
Dried oregano	5 ml	1 tsp	1 tsp
Can red kidney beans, drained	425 g	15 oz	1 large
Salt and black pepper			

TO SERVE
Boiled rice and salad

1   Fry (sauté) the onions in the oil for 3–4 minutes. Add the green pepper, carrots and garlic and continue cooking until the onions are soft but not brown. Stir in the cumin seeds and chilli to taste.

2   Add the remaining ingredients except the beans, bring to the boil, cover and cook for 30 minutes.

3   Add the beans and adjust the seasoning. Cook for a further 15 minutes. Serve with boiled rice and salad.

PREPARATION TIME: 15 MINUTES
COOKING TIME: 50 MINUTES

Chakchouka

SERVES 4	METRIC	IMPERIAL	AMERICAN
Large onion, chopped	1	1	1
Olive oil	45–60 ml	3–4 tbsp	3–4 tbsp
Garlic cloves, crushed	2	2	2
Green AND red (bell) peppers, cut into small pieces	½ each	½ each	½ each
Cauliflower, cut into florets	1	1	1
Tomatoes, skinned and chopped	450 g	1 lb	4 cups
Salt and pepper			
Paprika	10 ml	2 tsp	2 tsp
A good pinch of cayenne OR chilli powder			
Eggs	4	4	4

TO SERVE
Classic Potatoes with Cream (see page 131) and a green salad

1   Cook the onion in the oil for 5 minutes until soft. Add the garlic and cook for 1 minute.

2   Add the peppers, cauliflower and tomatoes. Season with salt and pepper, paprika and cayenne or chilli. Add a little water if necessary.

3   Cook over a low heat for about 20 minutes until the vegetables are tender, adding a little water if the mixture becomes dry.

4   Carefully break the eggs into the vegetable mixture, cover and cook until they are set, stir with a fork if liked or leave whole. Serve with Classic Potatoes with Cream and a green salad.

PREPARATION TIME: 10 MINUTES
COOKING TIME: 30 MINUTES

Vegetarian Hot Pot

*T*he topping of sliced potatoes makes this look really appetising. It would make a good topping for meat casseroles too.

SERVES 4	METRIC	IMPERIAL	AMERICAN
Large carrots, sliced	2	2	2
Small turnip, diced	1	1	1
Celery sticks, sliced	2	2	2
Butter	50 g	2 oz	¼ cup
Small leeks	12	12	12
Plain (all-purpose) flour	25 g	1 oz	¼ cup
Vegetable stock	450 ml	¾ pt	2 cups
Salt and pepper			
Worcestershire sauce	5 ml	1 tsp	1 tsp
Chopped parsley	30 ml	2 tbsp	2 tbsp
Potatoes, thinly sliced	450 g	1 lb	1 lb
Cheddar cheese, grated	50 g	2 oz	½ cup

TO GARNISH			
Chopped parsley			

1   Fry (sauté) the carrots, turnip and celery gently in the butter for 7–8 minutes and put into a casserole (Dutch oven).

2   Fry the leeks for 2–3 minutes until soft and put into the casserole.

3   Stir the flour into the pan and gradually add the stock. Bring to the boil, stirring. Season with salt and pepper and the Worcestershire sauce. Simmer for 3 minutes and mix in the parsley.

4   Pour over the vegetables in the casserole and turn them so they are thoroughly mixed.

5   Arrange the sliced potatoes in overlapping circles on top of the vegetables. Cover the casserole with a lid or foil and cook for 1½ hours at 180°C/350°F/gas mark 4 until the potatoes are tender.

6   Sprinkle the cheese over the potato topping and grill (broil) until browned. Serve garnished with parsley. This is a meal in itself, nothing else is necessary.

PREPARATION TIME: 15 MINUTES

COOKING TIME: 1¾ HOURS

Swiss Tomato Casserole

SERVES 4	METRIC	IMPERIAL	AMERICAN
Butter	40 g	1½ oz	3 tbsp
Milk	450 ml	¾ pt	2 cups
Plain (all-purpose) flour	40 g	1½ oz	⅓ cup
Salt and pepper			
Gruyère (Swiss) cheese, grated	100 g	4 oz	1 cup
Single (light) cream	60 ml	4 tbsp	4 tbsp
Firm tomatoes, sliced	750 g	1½ lb	1½ lb
Caster (superfine) sugar	10 ml	2 tsp	2 tsp
Chopped basil	5 ml	1 tsp	1 tsp
Grated Parmesan cheese	25 g	1 oz	¼ cup

TO GARNISH
Basil leaves

TO SERVE
Baked Sliced Potatoes (see page 135) and a green salad

1   Blend the butter, milk and flour and cook gently until thick. Add salt and pepper, the cheese and cream.

2   Layer the tomatoes and sauce in an ovenproof dish. Season with salt, pepper, sugar and basil as you go.

3   Sprinkle with Parmesan, cover and cook in the oven at 190°C/375°F/gas mark 5 for 30 minutes. Garnish with basil leaves. Serve with Baked Sliced Potatoes and a green salad.

PREPARATION TIME: 10 MINUTES
COOKING TIME: 35 MINUTES

Stuffed Courgettes

*D*espite the simple ingredients, it's surprising how rich and filling these courgettes are. They are also good if you substitute the cottage cheese with a soft cheese like Boursin.

SERVES 4	METRIC	IMPERIAL	AMERICAN
Sweetcorn (corn)	175 g	6 oz	1½ cups
Cottage cheese	100 g	4 oz	½ cup
Salt and pepper			
Shallots, finely chopped	2	2	2
Courgettes (zucchini), halved and seeds removed	4	4	4
Freshly grated Parmesan cheese	45 ml	3 tbsp	3 tbsp

TO SERVE
Baked Sliced Potatoes, Garlicky French Beans (see pages 135 and 144) or a green salad

1   Mix together the sweetcorn, cottage cheese, salt, pepper and shallots.

2   Spoon the mixture into the courgette halves, mounding it up a little. Top with the Parmesan cheese.

3   Put the courgettes into a greased shallow dish and bake for 15 minutes at 200°C/400°F/gas mark 6 until tender and the topping melts.

4   Serve with Baked Sliced Potatoes and Garlicky French Beans or a green salad.

PREPARATION TIME: 10 MINUTES
COOKING TIME: 15 MINUTES

Scalloped Aubergines

*T*his can be made in advance and just reheated. For a richer dish, add 1 egg beaten with 120 ml/4 fl oz/½ cup single (light) cream. Pour this mixture over the aubergines before baking.

SERVES 4	METRIC	IMPERIAL	AMERICAN
Aubergines (eggplants), diced	2	2	2
Butter, for greasing			
Onion, chopped	1	1	1
Garlic cloves, finely chopped	2	2	2
Olive oil	15 ml	1 tbsp	1 tbsp
Dried oregano	5 ml	1 tsp	1 tsp
Dried rosemary	5 ml	1 tsp	1 tsp
Salt	2.5 ml	½ tsp	½ tsp
Pepper	1.5 ml	¼ tsp	¼ tsp
Tomatoes, skinned and chopped OR a small can	4	4	4
Gruyère (Swiss) cheese, grated	100 g	4 oz	1 cup
TO SERVE			
Baked potatoes and salad			

1   Boil the aubergines in salted water for 1 minute. Drain and place to one side in a buttered dish.

2   Fry (sauté) the onion and garlic in the oil gently for 5 minutes. Spoon over the aubergines. Top with herbs, salt, pepper and tomatoes.

3   Bake for 25 minutes at 190°C/375°F/gas mark 5.

4   Sprinkle with the cheese and bake for a further 5
minutes until melted. Serve with baked potatoes and salad.

PREPARATION TIME: 10 MINUTES

COOKING TIME: 36 MINUTES

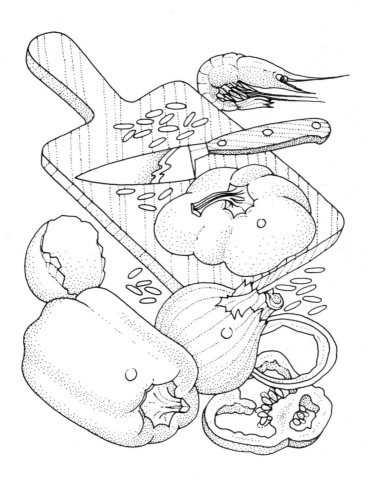

Vegetable Curry

This is a mild spicy curry for those who prefer subtle flavours. Serve chilled lager to drink rather than wine.

SERVES 4	METRIC	IMPERIAL	AMERICAN
Oil	30 ml	2 tbsp	2 tbsp
Ground coriander (cilantro)	10 ml	2 tsp	2 tsp
Ground cumin	5 ml	1 tsp	1 tsp
Chilli powder	2.5–5 ml	½–1 tsp	½–1 tsp
Turmeric	2.5 ml	½ tsp	½ tsp
Garlic cloves, crushed	2	2	2
Onion, chopped	1	1	1
Small cauliflower, cut into florets	1	1	1
Potatoes, chopped	2	2	2
Carrots, chopped	2	2	2
Green AND red (bell) pepper, chopped	½ each	½ each	½ each
Salt and pepper			
Tomatoes, chopped	225 g	8 oz	2 cups
Garam masala	5 ml	1 tsp	1 tsp
Plain yoghurt	150 ml	¼ pt	⅔ cup
TO SERVE			
Boiled rice, cucumber, banana, chutney and yoghurt			

1   Heat the oil, add the coriander, cumin, chilli, turmeric, garlic and onion and fry (sauté) for 2–3 minutes.

2   Add the cauliflower, potatoes, carrots, green and red pepper, salt and pepper and stir to coat with the spices.

3   Stir in the tomatoes and add 150 ml/¼ pt/⅔ cup water. Bring to the boil, cover and simmer for 30 minutes.

4   Add the garam masala. Remove from the heat and stir in the yoghurt.

5   Serve with rice and all the usual curry accompaniments: cucumber, banana, chutney and yoghurt.

PREPARATION TIME: 10 MINUTES

COOKING TIME: 35 MINUTES

Vegetarian Goulash

SERVES 4	METRIC	IMPERIAL	AMERICAN
Onion, finely chopped	1	1	1
Oil	30 ml	2 tbsp	2 tbsp
Courgette (zucchini), diced	1	1	1
Carrots, diced	225 g	8 oz	2 cups
Parsnips, diced	225 g	8 oz	2 cups
Celery sticks, sliced	2	2	2
Paprika	5 ml	1 tsp	1 tsp
Dried basil	2.5 ml	½ tsp	½ tsp
Caraway seeds	2.5 ml	½ tsp	½ tsp
Chopped parsley	30 ml	2 tbsp	2 tbsp
Marmite (yeast extract)	5 ml	1 tsp	1 tsp
Passata (sieved tomatoes)	600 ml	1 pt	2½ cups
Vegetable stock	450 ml	¾ pt	2 cups
Small potatoes	12	12	12
Plain yoghurt	150 ml	¼ pt	⅔ cup

TO SERVE
Ribbon noodles and Fried Peas with Garlic (see page 146)

1   Fry (sauté) the onion in the oil until soft but not brown. Add all the vegetables except the potatoes. Cover and cook for 10 minutes over a gentle heat.

2   Stir in the remaining ingredients except the yoghurt. Bring to the boil, simmer for 20–30 minutes.

3   Season to taste and stir in the yoghurt. Garnish with parsley. Serve with noodles and Fried Peas with Garlic.

PREPARATION TIME: 15 MINUTES
COOKING TIME: 25–35 MINUTES

Mushroom and Cashew Nut Pilaff

When I was trying out all the recipes before starting work in France, my brother Tim gave me this recipe. It has remained one of my favourites ever since I first tasted it.

SERVES 4	METRIC	IMPERIAL	AMERICAN
Brown rice	100 g	4 oz	1 cup
Onion, sliced	1	1	1
Oil			
Garlic clove, crushed	1	1	1
Celery sticks, sliced	2	2	2
Mushrooms, sliced	225 g	8 oz	4 cups
Red (bell) pepper, sliced	1	1	1
Green (bell) pepper, sliced	1	1	1
Cashew nuts	100 g	4 oz	1 cup
Soy sauce			

TO SERVE
Tomato and beansprout salad

1   Cook the rice according to the packet directions.

2   Fry (sauté) the onion in the oil for 5 minutes.

3   Add the garlic, celery, mushrooms, peppers and nuts. Mix together and fry for 2 minutes.

4   Add the soy sauce to taste, remembering that it is very salty. Fry for 5 minutes.

5   Add the cooked rice, mix together and heat through. Serve with a tomato and beansprout salad.

PREPARATION TIME: 10 MINUTES
COOKING TIME: 30 MINUTES

Side Dishes, Garnishes and Sauces

*I*t is obviously easier, in a way, to just serve plain boiled or steamed vegetables as side dishes. But your guests will be overwhelmed when you serve up these exciting combinations. What's more, most of them can be prepared in advance and either cooked along with the main course in the oven or simply reheated at the last minute in a pan or in the microwave. I have also included some clever ideas for garnishing vegetables and a few favourite sauces. If, however, you find the idea of elaborate veggies and main course too daunting, try, for a change, serving plain grilled chops or steaks (prettily garnished) with some exciting accompaniments.

Turkish Fried Carrots

*T*he middle-eastern flavour of these carrots is perfect with roast or grilled lamb or any plain grilled fish or meat.

SERVES 4	METRIC	IMPERIAL	AMERICAN
Carrots, sliced, lightly cooked and cooled	450 g	1 lb	1 lb
Seasoned flour	15 ml	1 tbsp	1 tbsp
Olive oil	30 ml	2 tbsp	2 tbsp
Salt and pepper			
Plain yoghurt	300 ml	½ pt	1¼ cups
A good pinch of garam masala			
TO GARNISH			
Chopped mint			

1 Spread the cooled, cooked carrots on to kitchen paper to dry. Toss them in the flour and shake off any surplus.

2 Fry (sauté) in the oil until golden brown. Season to taste. Keep warm on a serving dish. Put the yoghurt into a small pan and heat very gently. Pour over the carrots, sprinkle on the garam masala and garnish with mint.

PREPARATION TIME: 5 MINUTES PLUS COOKING TIME OF
    THE CARROTS

COOKING TIME: 5 MINUTES

Buttered Carrots and Parsley

ALLOW 1–2 CARROTS PER PERSON

*P*eel or scrape the carrots, slice them lengthwise into even-sized pieces. Boil until just tender. Toss in melted butter and serve sprinkled with chopped parsley.

Thyme and Parsley Carrots

*T*hese are particularly good with casseroles. If you use dried thyme, you'll need only 2.5 ml/½ tsp.

SERVES 8	METRIC	IMPERIAL	AMERICAN
Carrots, thinly sliced	1 kg	2¼ lb	2¼ lb
Soft brown sugar	10 ml	2 tsp	2 tsp
Butter	50 g	2 oz	¼ cup
Chopped thyme	10 ml	2 tsp	2 tsp
Chopped parsley	10 ml	2 tsp	2 tsp

1 Boil the carrots until tender in water with the sugar.

2 Drain off the liquid, stir in the butter and herbs and serve hot.

PREPARATION TIME: 10 MINUTES

COOKING TIME: 5–10 MINUTES

Creamy Courgette Bake

This is my all-time favourite courgette recipe and makes a wonderful creamy accompaniment to any plain meat or fish.

SERVES 4	METRIC	IMPERIAL	AMERICAN
Courgettes (zucchini), grated	450 g	1 lb	4 cups
Salt	5 ml	1 tsp	1 tsp
Caster (superfine) sugar	5 ml	1 tsp	1 tsp
Tarragon vinegar	10 ml	2 tsp	2 tsp
Butter, for greasing			
Egg, beaten	1	1	1
Thick (heavy) cream	300 ml	½ pt	1¼ cups
Basil leaves, torn	6	6	6
Grated Parmesan cheese	15 ml	1 tbsp	1 tbsp

1 Toss the courgettes with the salt, sugar and vinegar. Cover and leave in a cool place for several hours.

2 Drain the courgettes very well, squeezing them to get rid of all the juice – this is very important.

3 Put them in a lightly buttered gratin dish and fluff them up with a fork.

4 Beat the egg lightly with the cream, the torn basil leaves and the grated Parmesan. Pour over the courgettes. Bake at 200°C/400°F/gas mark 6 for about 20 minutes until the custard is set around the edges but still slightly creamy in the centre.

PREPARATION TIME: 5 MINUTES PLUS STANDING TIME

COOKING TIME: 20 MINUTES

Courgette Patties

*T*hese also make a delicious starter, served with either a tomato sauce or garlic and herb flavoured mayonnaise.

SERVES 4	METRIC	IMPERIAL	AMERICAN
Courgettes (zucchini), grated	275 g	10 oz	2½ cups
Plain (all-purpose) flour	40 g	1½ oz	⅓ cup
Eggs, lightly beaten	2	2	2
Salt	2.5 ml	½ tsp	½ tsp
A pinch of black pepper			
Butter	25 g	1 oz	2 tbsp
Oil	30 ml	2 tbsp	2 tbsp

1   Mix the courgettes with the flour, eggs, salt and a pinch of pepper to form a batter.

2   Fry (sauté) spoonfuls of the butter in hot butter and oil to form patties about 5 cm/2 in in diameter. Flatten each one slightly with the back of a spoon.

3   Cook them for about 4 minutes on each side until golden brown and crusty.

4   Transfer to a plate with kitchen paper to drain and keep warm. Keep frying the patties until all the batter is used up, adding more oil if needed. Serve hot.

PREPARATION TIME: 5 MINUTES
COOKING TIME: 8 MINUTES PER BATCH

Lemon Potatoes

I find these potatoes are particularly easy to cook for larger numbers of people (but the quantities can easily be reduced when necessary).

SERVES 8	METRIC	IMPERIAL	AMERICAN
Potatoes, cubed	1.75 kg	4 lb	4 lb
Butter	100 g	4 oz	½ cup
Onions, finely chopped	2	2	2
Grated rind and juice of 2 lemons			
Chopped parsley	60 ml	4 tbsp	4 tbsp
Salt and pepper			

1 Cover the potatoes with cold water, bring to the boil, simmer for 3 minutes and drain.

2 In the empty pan, melt the butter and add the onions and fry (sauté) until soft but not brown. Stir in the lemon rind and juice, parsley, salt and pepper.

3 Return the potatoes to the pan and toss gently to coat in the mixture. Put into a shallow ovenproof dish (they can be left like this all day in a cool place if needed).

4 Bake at 190°C/375°F/gas mark 5 for about 1 hour until they are golden brown and crispy on top.

PREPARATION TIME: 10 MINUTES
COOKING TIME: 1 HOUR 5 MINUTES

Sugar Browned Potatoes

*T*hese glazed potatoes are irresistible with any grilled meat or fish.

SERVES 4–6	METRIC	IMPERIAL	AMERICAN
Caster (superfine) sugar	25 g	1 oz	2 tbsp
Unsalted butter	50 g	2 oz	¼ cup
Small potatoes, cooked and drained	900 g	2 lb	2 lb

1   Heat the sugar and butter in a frying pan (skillet) until caramelised.

2   Rinse the potatoes in cold water before adding to the frying pan. Continue cooking over a low heat, shaking the pan gently, until the potatoes are evenly glazed and golden brown. Serve hot.

PREPARATION AND COOKING TIME: 25 MINUTES

Mustard Roast Potatoes

*T*oss par-boiled potatoes in mustard powder, then roast as usual for 1 hour.

Fantailed Roast Potatoes

*C*ut three-quarters of the way through the par-boiled potatoes at 3 mm/⅛ in intervals. Roast for about 45 minutes in a hot oven.

Classic Potatoes with Cream

This is a combination of various potato recipes cooked in the oven with cream. It is delicious with any plain meat or fish dish which requires a moist vegetable. You can make as little or as much as you like – allow at least 1 potato per person.

Slice the potatoes thinly and sprinkle with salt. Leave for 5–10 minutes and then squeeze out excess water. Butter a shallow ovenproof dish and rub it with a crushed garlic clove. Layer the potatoes in the dish, sprinkle with nutmeg and pepper between each layer, and pour enough UHT cream to reach the top layer. Top with dots of butter. Bake uncovered at 140°C/275°F/gas mark 1 for at least 1 hour (preferably longer).

To microwave: Cover with microwave film and cook for 30 minutes (at least) on low – this depends on the power of your microwave. It is best to get them going early. If ready early, just remove from the oven and reheat later. Grill (broil) the potatoes until golden brown on top before serving.

Note:

If making a large quantity, use a large shallow dish. Do not be tempted to make the layers too deep, or it will take too long to cook through.

PREPARATION TIME: 10 MINUTES PLUS SALTING TIME

COOKING TIME: AT LEAST 1 HOUR IN THE OVEN,
30 MINUTES IN THE MICROWAVE

Swedish Potatoes

*T*hese potatoes are traditionally served with a plate of smoked salmon, but they are delicious served as an accompaniment to any fish – especially smoked varieties.

SERVES 4	METRIC	IMPERIAL	AMERICAN
New potatoes, scraped	750 g	1½ lb	1½ lb
Olive oil	15 ml	1 tbsp	1 tbsp
Butter	25 g	1 oz	2 tbsp
Plain (all-purpose) flour	40 g	1½ oz	⅓ cup
Milk	300 ml	½ pt	1¼ cups
Dried dill (dill weed)	5 ml	1 tsp	1 tsp
Dill seed	5 ml	1 tsp	1 tsp
Finely chopped parsley	15 ml	1 tbsp	1 tbsp
Salt and pepper			
Lemon juice	30 ml	2 tbsp	2 tbsp

1   Place the potatoes in a pan of boiling, lightly salted water. Add the oil. Bring back to the boil and cook until the potatoes are tender. Drain and keep warm.

2   Melt the butter in a saucepan and blend in the flour. Gradually add the milk, stirring constantly. Add the dried dill and dill seed and cook, stirring, until it starts to thicken. Add the parsley, seasoning and lemon juice.

3   Beat the sauce well and add the potatoes. Heat through for 2 minutes, then turn into a warmed dish and serve.

PREPARATION TIME: 10 MINUTES
COOKING TIME: 20 MINUTES

Antibes Potatoes

SERVES 3–4	METRIC	IMPERIAL	AMERICAN
Potatoes, scrubbed	450 g	1 lb	1 lb
Oil for roasting			
Salt and pepper			
Chopped herbs	15 ml	1 tbsp	1 tbsp

1 Cut the potatoes into big chips and boil them until they are nearly cooked. Drain and put into a roasting tin (pan).

2 Drizzle over enough oil to just coat the chips. Season with salt, pepper and herbs. Toss lightly. Bake in the oven at 230°C/450°F/gas mark 8 for about 20 minutes until golden brown.

PREPARATION TIME: 5 MINUTES PLUS PAR-BOILING

COOKING TIME: 20 MINUTES

French Beans with Onions and Garlic

SERVES 4	METRIC	IMPERIAL	AMERICAN
Green beans	450 g	1 lb	1 lb
Small onion, finely chopped	1	1	1
Garlic clove, crushed	1	1	1
Butter	25 g	1 oz	2 tbsp

1 Cook the green beans in boiling, lightly salted water until just tender.

2 Fry (sauté) the onion until soft but not brown. Add garlic and cook for 30 seconds. Do not allow to brown.

3 Drain the beans, toss with the onion mix and serve.

PREPARATION AND COOKING TIME: 10 MINUTES

Galettes

*R*ich and satisfying and rather good as a light main course as well as an unusual vegetable accompaniment.

SERVES 6	METRIC	IMPERIAL	AMERICAN
Old potatoes	900 g	2 lb	2 lb
Celeriac (celery root)	900 g	2 lb	2 lb
Garlic clove, crushed	1	1	1
A pinch of grated nutmeg			
Salt and pepper			
Butter, melted	75 g	3 oz	¼ cup
TO GARNISH			
Sprigs of parsley			

1   Thinly slice the potatoes and celeriac, preferably in a food processor or with a mandolin. Grease and line two 20 cm/8 in sandwich tins (pans) with baking parchment.

2   Layer the sliced vegetables with the garlic, nutmeg, and seasoning. Press down firmly after each layer.

3   Pour about half of the melted butter over each tin.

4   Cover with foil and bake at 230°C/450°F/gas mark 8 for 1¼ hours until the vegetables are tender when tested with a skewer. Turn out on to serving dishes and garnish with parsley.

PREPARATION TIME: 10 MINUTES
COOKING TIME: 1¼ HOURS

Baked Sliced Potatoes

*S*imple and yet so much tastier than plain roast potatoes – especially if your meat part of the meal is plain cooked.

SERVES 4	METRIC	IMPERIAL	AMERICAN
Potatoes, sliced thinly	4	4	4
Olive oil	45 ml	3 tbsp	3 tbsp
Salt	5 ml	1 tsp	1 tsp
Black pepper	2.5 ml	½ tsp	½ tsp
Mixed dried herbs	2.5 ml	½ tsp	½ tsp

1   Mix the potatoes with the other ingredients.

2   Cook in a large flat dish for about 20–30 minutes at 220°C/425°F/gas mark 7, until the potatoes are crispy at the edges.

PREPARATION TIME: 5 MINUTES

COOKING TIME: 20–30 MINUTES

Stir-fried Vegetables

*S*tir-fried vegetables, especially a combination of vegetables, make a lovely bright accompaniment to many dishes, not just Chinese ones. Remember to keep the oil hot. Work quickly and start with the firmest vegetables, toss in a little oil then add the next, finishing with the softest. Add a dash of soy sauce and sherry, and a pinch of sugar, ground ginger, salt and pepper.

Choose any mixture: carrots, celery, (bell) peppers, mushrooms, cucumber, courgettes (zucchini), etc. Cut into even-sized strips or slices.

PREPARATION AND COOKING TIME: ABOUT 20 MINUTES
(DEPENDING ON QUANTITIES)

Creamed Spinach

SERVES 6	METRIC	IMPERIAL	AMERICAN
Unsalted (sweet) butter	50 g	2 oz	¼ cup
Frozen leaf spinach, thawed and drained	1 kg	2¼ lb	2¼ lb
Garlic cloves, crushed	2	2	2
A good pinch of grated nutmeg			
Salt			
Black pepper			
Double (heavy) cream	120 ml	4 fl oz	½ cup

1   Melt the butter, add the drained spinach, garlic, plenty of nutmeg, a little salt and a generous grinding of pepper.

2   Gradually add enough cream to give the spinach a creamy consistency. Gently heat through and serve.

PREPARATION AND COOKING TIME: 5 MINUTES

Zingy Carrots and Courgettes

SERVES 4	METRIC	IMPERIAL	AMERICAN
Oil	15 ml	1 tbsp	1 tbsp
Butter	25 g	1 oz	2 tbsp
Courgettes (zucchini), grated	2	2	2
Carrots, grated	2	2	2
Garlic cloves, crushed	2	2	2
Grated rind of 1 lime			
Salt and pepper			
Juice of ½ lime			
Dried thyme	5 ml	1 tsp	1 tsp

1   In a large frying pan (skillet), heat the oil and butter. Add the grated vegetables and garlic and fry (sauté) for 2 minutes.

2   Add the lime rind and season to taste. Stir in the juice and thyme and continue to cook for a further 5–6 minutes. Serve hot.

PREPARATION TIME: 10 MINUTES (LESS WITH A FOOD
    PROCESSOR)

COOKING TIME: 8 MINUTES

Orange Ginger Carrots

SERVES 4	METRIC	IMPERIAL	AMERICAN
Carrots, thinly sliced	450 g	1 lb	4 cups
Sugar	10 ml	2 tsp	2 tsp
Cornflour (cornstarch)	5 ml	1 tsp	1 tsp
Salt	1.5 ml	¼ tsp	¼ tsp
Ground ginger	1.5 ml	¼ tsp	¼ tsp
Orange juice	60 ml	4 tbsp	4 tbsp
Butter	15 g	½ oz	1 tbsp

1   Cook the carrots until almost tender but still with a little 'bite'. Drain and return to the pan.

2   Mix the sugar, cornflour, salt, ginger and orange juice. Add to the carrots, bring to the boil, stirring.

3   Add the butter, toss well and serve.

PREPARATION TIME: 10 MINUTES

COOKING TIME: 10 MINUTES

Mushroom and Wild Rice Pilaff

*T*his makes a very good light main course as well as being the perfect accompaniment to grills and casseroles.

SERVES 6	METRIC	IMPERIAL	AMERICAN
Large onion, chopped	1	1	1
Mushrooms, sliced	750 g	1½ lb	12 cups
Garlic clove, crushed	1	1	1
Sunflower oil	60 ml	4 tbsp	4 tbsp
Long-grain rice	225 g	8 oz	1 cup
Wild rice	30 ml	2 tbsp	2 tbsp
Vegetable stock	600 ml	1 pt	2½ cups
Dried mixed herbs	10 ml	2 tsp	2 tsp
Salt and black pepper			

1   Fry (sauté) the onion, mushrooms and garlic in the oil. When the onion is soft, add the long-grain and wild rice and stir around to absorb the flavours.

2   Pour in the stock, add the herbs and seasoning. Cover and simmer for about 20 minutes so that the liquid is absorbed and the rice is just tender. Fluff up with a fork and serve.

PREPARATION TIME: 5 MINUTES
COOKING TIME: 25 MINUTES

Garlic Cabbage

This is particularly good with pork dishes (even sausages take on a new lease of life!).

SERVES 4	METRIC	IMPERIAL	AMERICAN
Small head of cabbage	1	1	1
Garlic cloves, sliced finely	2	2	2
Unsalted (sweet) butter	50 g	2 oz	¼ cup
Salt	2.5 ml	½ tsp	½ tsp
Black pepper	1.5 ml	¼ tsp	¼ tsp

TO GARNISH			
Red (bell) pepper, thinly sliced			

1   Quarter the cabbage and then slice thinly, discarding the core. Add the cabbage and garlic to the melted butter and fry (sauté) for about 1 minute.

2   Cover the pan and cook very gently for about 15 minutes so that the cabbage is cooked but still crisp. Season with salt and pepper.

3   Garnish with thinly sliced red pepper.

PREPARATION AND COOKING TIME: 20 MINUTES

Pasta with Vegetable Ribbons

*T*he carrot and courgette add colour to this pasta dish. For extra flavour, add a small pared parsnip

SERVES 4	METRIC	IMPERIAL	AMERICAN
Tagliatelle	225 g	8 oz	½ lb
Carrot, pared into ribbons with a swivel peeler	1	1	1
Courgette (zucchini), pared into ribbons with a swivel peeler	1	1	1
Butter	15 g	½ oz	1 tbsp

1 Cook the pasta according to packet directions.

2 1 minute before the end of cooking time, add the carrot ribbons and then the courgettes. Drain, toss in butter and serve.

PREPARATION AND COOKING TIME: 10 MINUTES

Cauliflower with Almonds

SERVES 4	METRIC	IMPERIAL	AMERICAN
Large cauliflower, cut into florets	1	1	1
Salt			
Flaked almonds	50 g	2 oz	½ cup
Unsalted (sweet) butter	50 g	2 oz	½ cup

1 Boil or steam the cauliflower until almost tender (but not soft). Drain, if necessary, and season very lightly with salt (if liked).

2   Fry (sauté) the almonds in the butter until brown.
Spoon over the cooked cauliflower and serve.

PREPARATION TIME: 5 MINUTES
COOKING TIME: 8–10 MINUTES

Carrots with Orange and Cardamom

SERVES 4–6	METRIC	IMPERIAL	AMERICAN
Baby carrots, topped and tailed	750 g	1½ lb	1½ lb
Thick plain yoghurt	150 ml	¼ pt	⅔ cup
Juice of 1 large orange			
Green cardamoms, crushed	3	3	3
Olive oil	30 ml	2 tbsp	2 tbsp
Salt and pepper			

1   Steam the carrots for 10–12 minutes until just tender.
Turn them into a deep dish.

2   Mix the yoghurt, orange juice, cardamom seeds and
olive oil with a pinch of salt and pepper and quickly stir the
mixture into the carrots. Serve hot, warm or cold.

PREPARATION TIME: 8 MINUTES
COOKING TIME: 10–12 MINUTES

Orange Glazed Turnips

*T*hese orangy turnips go particularly well with rich meats like lamb, pork or duck.

SERVES 4	METRIC	IMPERIAL	AMERICAN
Baby turnips, left whole	750 g	1½ lb	1½ lb
Butter	75 g	3 oz	⅓ cup
Sugar	30 ml	2 tbsp	2 tbsp
Large red onion, cut into wedges	1	1	1
Oranges, peeled and cut into segments	2	2	2
TO GARNISH			
Snipped chives			

1 Cook the turnips in boiling salted water for 10 minutes until tender, then drain.

2 Melt the butter and stir in the sugar, until dissolved.

3 Add the turnips and cook for 6–8 minutes over a high heat, stirring now and then. Add the onion and oranges and cook for a further 5 minutes. Serve hot, garnished with snipped chives.

PREPARATION TIME: 10 MINUTES
COOKING TIME: 25 MINUTES

Cauliflower Sautéed with Coriander

$\mathcal{T}$he garlic and coriander add a new dimension to an otherwise rather bland vegetable.

SERVES 2–4	METRIC	IMPERIAL	AMERICAN
Small cauliflower	1	1	1
Onion, finely chopped	½	½	½
Olive oil	30 ml	2 tbsp	2 tbsp
Coriander (cilantro) seeds, crushed	5 ml	1 tsp	1 tsp
Salt and pepper			
Butter	15 ml	½ oz	1 tbsp
Small garlic clove, crushed	1	1	1

1   Separate the cauliflower into small florets. Do not wash, but wipe if necessary.

2   Soften the onion in the oil in a large frying pan (skillet). Turn up the heat and add the cauliflower florets and keep turning them over.

3   After 2 minutes, add the crushed coriander seeds and continue cooking for about 5 minutes.

4   Season, add the butter and garlic and cook for a further 1–2 minutes until golden brown but still crunchy.

PREPARATION TIME: 5 MINUTES
COOKING TIME: 14–15 MINUTES

Broccoli with Garlic and Mustard Seeds

SERVES 6	METRIC	IMPERIAL	AMERICAN
Broccoli, cut into equal sized spears	900 g	2 lb	2 lb
Yellow mustard seeds	10 ml	2 tsp	2 tsp
Olive oil	75 ml	5 tbsp	5 tbsp
Garlic cloves, crushed	2–3	2–3	2–3
Salt	2.5 ml	½ tsp	½ tsp

1   Steam the broccoli spears until just tender, then rinse immediately in cold water.

2   Just before serving, fry (sauté) the mustard seeds in the oil. When they pop, stir in the garlic.

3   Add the spears and salt. Stir gently to mix and cook until heated through and glistening.

PREPARATION AND COOKING TIME: 10 MINUTES

Garlicky French Beans

*T*hese beans also make an unusual starter, served with sun-dried tomato Ciabatta bread.

SERVES 4	METRIC	IMPERIAL	AMERICAN
Green beans	450 g	1 lb	1 lb
Small onion, finely chopped	1	1	1
Garlic clove, crushed	1	1	1
Butter	25 g	1 oz	2 tbsp

1   Boil the beans in lightly salted water.

2   Fry (sauté) the onion in the butter until soft but not brown. Add garlic and cook for a further 30 seconds.

3   Drain the beans and toss with the onion mixture before serving.

PREPARATION AND COOKING TIME: 10 MINUTES

Brussels Sprouts with Almonds

SERVES 4	METRIC	IMPERIAL	AMERICAN
Sprouts, trimmed, with a small cross cut in the stalks	450 g	1 lb	1 lb
Flaked almonds	25 g	1 oz	¼ cup
Butter	25 g	1 oz	2 tbsp
Olive oil	15 ml	1 tbsp	1 tbsp
Black pepper			

1   Boil the sprouts in salted water for about 5 minutes until tender. Drain.

2   Meanwhile, fry (sauté) the almonds until golden in the butter and oil. Season with pepper. Pour over the sprouts, toss gently and serve.

PREPARATION TIME: 10 MINUTES

COOKING TIME: 5 MINUTES

French Style Green Beans

*T*his is an unusual, but very simple, way to add interest to green beans. It is equally delicious with peas.

SERVES 4	METRIC	IMPERIAL	AMERICAN
Green beans	450 g	1 lb	1 lb
Rashers (slices) streaky bacon, cut into pieces	2	2	2
Butter	50 g	2 oz	2 oz
Spring onions (scallions), chopped	6	6	6
Lettuce leaves, shredded	8	8	8
Salt, pepper and a pinch of sugar			
TO GARNISH			
Chopped mint or parsley			

1   Par-boil the beans first, then drain.

2   Cook the bacon in the butter. Add the spring onions, beans, lettuce and seasoning. Cover and continue cooking, stirring occasionally, until the beans are tender. Serve garnished with mint or parsley.

PREPARATION TIME: 5 MINUTES
COOKING TIME: 10 MINUTES

Fried Peas and Garlic

(QUANTITIES TO SUIT TASTE)

Fry (sauté) frozen peas in plenty of butter. After 2 minutes add a little sugar, lots of black pepper and crushed garlic to taste. Cover and cook gently until the peas are tender – about 5 minutes.

146

Artichoke and Potato Bake

*A*s a main meal this will serve 3 people, or 6 if eaten as an accompaniment.

SERVES 3–6	METRIC	IMPERIAL	AMERICAN
Potatoes, thinly sliced	750 g	1½ lb	1½ lb
Can artichoke bottoms, drained and thinly sliced	400 g	14 oz	1 large
Garlic cloves, crushed	2	2	2
Chopped thyme	30 ml	2 tbsp	2 tbsp
Salt and pepper			
Double (heavy) cream	150 ml	¼ pt	⅔ cup
Milk	450 ml	¾ pt	2 cups
Unsalted (sweet) butter	25 g	1 oz	2 tbsp

1   Layer the potatoes and artichokes with the garlic, thyme and seasoning in a shallow ovenproof dish. Top with a layer of potato slices.

2   Mix the cream and milk together and pour over the top of the layers. Dot with the butter.

3   Bake for 1½–1¾ hours at 180°C/350°F/gas mark 4 until the potatoes are tender and most of the liquid has been absorbed.

PREPARATION TIME: 10 MINUTES
COOKING TIME: 1½–1¾ HOURS

Broccoli and Potato Bake

*T*his is a really easy and versatile recipe. You can serve it as a main course too and it tastes just as good if boiled leeks are used instead of the broccoli.

SERVES 4	METRIC	IMPERIAL	AMERICAN
Double (heavy) cream	150 ml	¼ pt	⅔ cup
Gruyère (Swiss) cheese, grated	75 g	3 oz	¾ cup
Salt and pepper			
Broccoli, cooked until just tender	225 g	8 oz	½ lb
Potatoes, boiled and sliced	750 g	1½ lb	1½ lb

1 Mix the cream with half the cheese and add salt and pepper to taste. Place the broccoli and then the potatoes in a shallow flameproof dish.

2 Top with the cream mixture and finally the remaining cheese.

3 Cook under a hot grill (broiler) for about 5 minutes until the top is bubbling and golden brown. If you are using cold ingredients, reheat in the oven at 200°C/400°F/gas mark 6 for about 25 minutes.

PREPARATION TIME: 15 MINUTES (INCLUDING COOKING POTATOES AND BROCCOLI)

COOKING TIME: 5 MINUTES (OR 25 MINUTES IF FROM COLD)

Re-fried Beans

This recipe is a variation of the re-fried beans eaten with chilli beef and tortillas, but this recipe uses white beans. Until you try them, I don't think you'll be able to imagine just how delectable they are.

SERVES 3–4	METRIC	IMPERIAL	AMERICAN
Can haricot (navy) beans, drained, rinsed and drained again	425 g	15 oz	1 large
Olive oil	60 ml	4 tbsp	4 tbsp
Garlic cloves, crushed	2	2	2
Black pepper and salt			
TO GARNISH			
Chopped coriander (cilantro) or parsley			

1 Put all the ingredients into a shallow frying pan (skillet) and cook over a low heat, stirring to blend them all together. When heated through, continue cooking for a further 5–6 minutes so that the beans become a bit mushy.

2 Serve, garnished with chopped coriander or parsley.

PREPARATION TIME: 2 MINUTES
COOKING TIME: 10 MINUTES

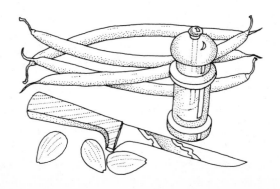

French Beans with Feta and Sun-dried Tomatoes

*F*or this recipe use sun-dried tomatoes packed in oil for a full, rich flavour.

SERVES 6	METRIC	IMPERIAL	AMERICAN
Frozen French beans	350 g	12 oz	¾ lb
Sun-dried tomatoes, cut into slices	50 g	2 oz	½ cup
Feta cheese, crumbled	100 g	4 oz	1 cup
Pepper and a little salt			
Oil from the tomatoes	15 ml	1 tbsp	1 tbsp

1   Cook the beans as directed on the packet. Drain.

2   Toss together with the remaining ingredients over a gentle heat. Serve immediately.

PREPARATION AND COOKING TIME: 10 MINUTES

Soy Garlic Beans

*T*he Oriental flavour of these beans goes very well with Mediterranean meat and fish dishes.

SERVES 4	METRIC	IMPERIAL	AMERICAN
Frozen green beans	450 g	1 lb	1 lb
Sunflower oil	15 ml	1 tbsp	1 tbsp
Butter, softened	15 ml	1 tbsp	1 tbsp
Garlic cloves, chopped	2	2	2
Soy sauce	15 ml	1 tbsp	1 tbsp
A pinch of sugar			
Water	250 ml	8 fl oz	1 cup

1 Fry (sauté) the beans in the oil and butter for 3 minutes.

2 Sprinkle the garlic, soy sauce and sugar over the beans and pour over the water. Bring to the boil and boil rapidly until the liquid has evaporated. Serve at once.

PREPARATION AND COOKING TIME: 10 MINUTES

Baked Fennel and Tomatoes

*T*hese casseroled vegetables with their juicy sauce are an ideal accompaniment to grilled meat or fish.

SERVES 4	METRIC	IMPERIAL	AMERICAN
Garlic cloves, peeled	6	6	6
Olive oil, plus extra for roasting	30 ml	2 tbsp	2 tbsp
Fennel bulbs, thickly sliced	750 g	1½ lb	1½ lb
Plain (all-purpose) flour	60 ml	4 tbsp	4 tbsp
Juicy tomatoes, cut into quarters	450 g	1 lb	1 lb
Sugar	10 ml	2 tsp	2 tsp
Salt and pepper			
Dried thyme	10 ml	2 tsp	2 tsp

1   Fry (sauté) the garlic in the oil until browned and transfer to a casserole dish (Dutch oven).

2   Coat the fennel with flour and fry until golden.

3   Add a little more oil and the tomatoes, sugar and seasoning. When bubbling, turn into the dish with the garlic. Sprinkle with the thyme, cover and cook for 1 hour at 180°C/350°F/gas mark 4.

COOKING TIME: 1 HOUR

Festive Sweet and Sour Onions

hese tender little onions make an interesting change from the usual Christmas vegetables.

SERVES 6	METRIC	IMPERIAL	AMERICAN
Button (pearl) onions, peeled	1 kg	2¼ lb	2¼ lb
Passata (sieved tomatoes)	400 ml	14 fl oz	1¾ cups
Soft brown sugar	100 g	4 oz	½ cup
Olive oil	30 ml	2 tbsp	2 tbsp
Red wine vinegar	60 ml	4 tbsp	4 tbsp
Dried thyme	2.5 ml	½ tsp	½ tsp
Pepper			

1   Blanch the onions for 10 minutes in boiling salted water. If you are using a bag of frozen onions, then this blanching is not necessary. Drain and tip into a shallow ovenproof dish.

2   Mix all the other ingredients together and pour over the onions. Bake in the oven at 180°C/350°F/gas mark 4 for 1 hour, basting occasionally.

PREPARATION TIME: 5 MINUTES PLUS ONION BLANCHING
     TIME

COOKING TIME: 1 HOUR

Mustard Turnips

 urnips have the reputation of being rather dull, but cooking them like this gives them a lovely buttery taste.

SERVES 6	METRIC	IMPERIAL	AMERICAN
Baby turnips, left whole	900 g	2 lb	2 lb
Unsalted (sweet) butter	50 g	2 oz	¼ cup
Chicken stock	150 ml	¼ pt	⅔ cup
Soft brown sugar	5 ml	1 tsp	1 tsp
Salt and black pepper			
French mustard	10 ml	2 tsp	2 tsp
Finely chopped parsley	30 ml	2 tbsp	2 tbsp

1 Fry (sauté) the turnips in the butter, coating them well.
Continue to cook over a moderate heat for about 10 minutes
so that they turn an even golden colour, like roast potatoes.

2 Add the stock, sprinkle with sugar and season to taste.
Bring to the boil, reduce the heat, cover and simmer for 20
minutes, shaking occasionally until tender.

3 Remove them from the pan and stir the mustard into
the pan juices, adding more sugar or seasoning if necessary.
Return the turnips to the pan, reheat them and swirl around
to coat in the buttery glaze. Serve garnished with the parsley.

PREPARATION TIME: 5 MINUTES
COOKING TIME: 35 MINUTES

Anchovy Cream

This dressing is sufficient for 750 g/1½ lb new potatoes, or you can use it as a sauce for pouring over simple grilled salmon. Even though there is a whole can of anchovies in the recipe, the finished cream has only a very subtle hint of fish.

SERVES 6	METRIC	IMPERIAL	AMERICAN
Can anchovy fillets in oil, chopped	50 g	2 oz	1 small
Double (heavy) cream	150 ml	¼ pt	⅔ cup
Black pepper			
Snipped chives	30 ml	2 tbsp	2 tbsp

1   Put the anchovies in their oil into a bowl over a pan of simmering water and stir until they form a smooth paste.

2   Pour the cream into another pan and slowly bring to the boil, simmer for 3–4 minutes. Remove from the heat, add the anchovy paste then leave to cool. Season to taste with pepper, add the chives and use as required.

PREPARATION AND COOKING TIME: 10 MINUTES

Anchovy Vinaigrette

*T*his dressing is particularly good with hard-boiled (hard-cooked) eggs and juicy tomatoes, but is excellent with green beans or a simple green salad too. The quantities here will make 150 ml/¼ pt/⅔ cup.

	METRIC	IMPERIAL	AMERICAN
Salt and black pepper			
Anchovy essence (extract)	2.5 ml	½ tsp	½ tsp
French mustard	5 ml	1 tsp	1 tsp
Wine vinegar	15 ml	1 tbsp	1 tbsp
Olive oil	75 ml	5 tbsp	5 tbsp

Whisk all the ingredients except the oil until blended. Gradually whisk in the oil. Use as required.

PREPARATION TIME: 2 MINUTES

Leek and Honey Sauce

*T*his sauce is a delicious accompaniment to any lamb dish, especially Rosemary Roasted Lamb Fillets (see page 76). Stir any meat juices into the sauce before serving.

SERVES 6	METRIC	IMPERIAL	AMERICAN
Leeks, finely chopped	350 g	12 oz	¾ lb
Unsalted (sweet) butter	50 g	2 oz	¼ cup
Plain (all-purpose) flour	15 ml	1 tbsp	1 tbsp
Chicken stock	300 ml	½ pt	1¼ cups
White wine	75 ml	5 tbsp	5 tbsp
White wine vinegar	30 ml	2 tbsp	2 tbsp
Clear honey	30 ml	2 tbsp	2 tbsp
Chopped parsley	30 ml	2 tbsp	2 tbsp
Salt and pepper			

1   Fry (sauté) the leeks in the butter gently for about 5 minutes until soft, but not brown.

2   Add the flour and cook for 1 minute. Stir in the stock, wine, vinegar and honey.

3   Bring to the boil and simmer for 3 minutes. Stir in the parsley and seasoning and serve.

PREPARATION TIME: 5 MINUTES

COOKING TIME: 9 MINUTES

Pesto

*P*esto can be added to a variety of dishes to give an Italian flavour and is readily available in most super-markets. However, it is really easy to make, especially if you grow your own basil. You can vary the flavour by adding 30 ml/2 tbsp freshly grated Parmesan cheese or chopped sun-dried tomatoes. It is delicious stirred into hot pasta as an instant sauce or mixed with soft cheese for a quick tasty dip. This recipe makes about 300 ml/½ pt/1¼ cups.

	METRIC	IMPERIAL	AMERICAN
Large bunch of basil leaves	1	1	1
Garlic cloves	3	3	3
Pine nuts	50 g	2 oz	½ cup
Salt	1.5 ml	¼ tsp	¼ tsp
Black pepper	1.5 ml	¼ tsp	¼ tsp
Olive oil	150 ml	¼ pt	⅔ cup

Purée all the ingredients together in a food processor or blender until smooth. The sauce can be kept in the fridge in a screw topped jar for 10 days.

PREPARATION TIME: 5 MINUTES

Garnishes for Vegetables

When time is of the essence, any of these can turn plain cooked vegetables into a masterpiece.

- Apricot jam (conserve) stirred into cooked carrots gives a lovely fruity taste.

- Parsley and melted butter are excellent for carrots, potatoes and sweetcorn (corn) kernels.

- Orange cordial is good for tossing carrots and leeks in.

- Onions fried (sautéed) until soft but not brown are good with peas and beans.

- Browned fried (sautéed) onions are good with cauliflower.

- Fried (sautéed) or toasted nuts and/or raisins are excellent with sprouts, cauliflower, courgettes (zucchini), broccoli and rice.

- Chopped bacon, fried (sautéed) until crisp is a good addition to peas, beans, leeks and also salad.

- Very thinly sliced red (bell) pepper adds bright colour to green vegetables.

- Tomatoes stewed with herbs are a good mix for green beans and cauliflower.

- Fried (sautéed) mushrooms make peas and sweetcorn (corn) a bit more unusual.

- Cream cheese and egg yolks make mashed potatoes taste rich and elegant.

- Cream, garlic and a hint of nutmeg transform spinach into a delight.

Desserts

No dinner party would be complete without a dessert. As a rule, if I am entertaining six or more guests, I offer a choice of sweets. I always make sure they are totally different in colour, texture and flavour. The trouble is most people opt for a bit of both – so don't be too generous when giving the first portions!

Mandarin and Chocolate Cheesecake

SERVES 6	METRIC	IMPERIAL	AMERICAN
Butter, melted	50 g	2 oz	¼ cup
Chocolate digestive biscuits (graham crackers), crushed	200 g	7 oz	1¾ cups
Can mandarin oranges	350 g	12 oz	1 large
Powdered gelatine	15 g	½ oz	1 tbsp
Mascarpone cheese	225 g	8 oz	1 cup
Eggs, separated	2	2	2
Caster (superfine) sugar	75 g	3 oz	⅓ cup
Crème fraîche OR soured (dairy sour) cream	150 ml	¼ pt	⅔ cup
Orange liqueur	30 ml	2 tbsp	2 tbsp
Juice and grated rind of 1 tangerine			

TO DECORATE
Grated chocolate

1   Mix together the butter with the biscuit crumbs and press into the base of a 20 cm/8 in flan dish (pie pan) or spring form cake tin (pan). Leave to chill while making the filling.

2   Drain the mandarins. Finely chop. Sprinkle the tangerine juice over the gelatine and leave to soften. Heat gently to dissolve.

3   Beat together the cheese, egg yolks, 50 g/2 oz/¼ cup of the sugar, the crème fraîche and the liqueur.

4   Stir in the gelatine, tangerine rind and mandarin pieces.

5   Whisk the egg whites until stiff and then whisk in the remaining sugar. Fold this into the cheese mixture and spoon over the biscuit base. Chill for 3–4 hours to set before decorating with grated chocolate.

PREPARATION TIME: 20 MINUTES PLUS CHILLING TIME

White Chocolate Mousse

SERVES 6	METRIC	IMPERIAL	AMERICAN
White chocolate	225 g	8 oz	½ lb
Unsalted (sweet) butter	25 g	1 oz	2 tbsp
Eggs, separated	5	5	5

TO DECORATE
Mixed white and dark grated chocolate

1   Gently melt the chocolate with the butter in a microwave or in a bowl over a pan of hot water.

2   Gradually add the egg yolks.

3   Whisk the egg whites until stiff and fold the chocolate mixture into the whites. Pour into 6 ramekins (custard cups) and chill until set. Decorate with a sprinkling of white and dark grated chocolate before serving.

PREPARATION TIME: 6 MINUTES PLUS CHILLING TIME

Chocolate Amaretti Creams

*T*hese sumptuous little tortes are deceptively quick and easy to make and can be made well in advance and left in the fridge until the evening.

SERVES 4	METRIC	IMPERIAL	AMERICAN
Amaretti biscuits (cookies), crushed	4	4	4
Plain (semi-sweet) chocolate	250 g	9 oz	good ½ lb
Amaretto liqueur	30 ml	2 tbsp	2 tbsp
Glycerine	30 ml	2 tbsp	2 tbsp
Double (heavy) cream	300 ml	½ pt	1½ cups

TO SERVE			
Single (light) cream			

1 Line the bases of 4 ramekin dishes (custard cups) with greaseproof (waxed) paper and divide the crushed amaretti biscuits between the dishes.

2 Gently melt the chocolate with the liqueur and glycerine in the microwave or in a bowl over a pan of hot water and allow to cool slightly. Whip the cream until softly peaking.

3 Stir 30 ml/2 tbsp of the cream into the chocolate mixture to soften it, then add the rest of the cream and fold in until well blended.

4 Pour into the ramekins and level the surfaces. Chill for at least 45 minutes.

5 To serve: run a knife around the edge of each ramekin, cover with a serving plate and invert on to the plate, remove the paper and serve with a jug of single cream.

PREPARATION TIME: 15 MINUTES PLUS CHILLING TIME

Almond Pear Flan

SERVES 6	METRIC	IMPERIAL	AMERICAN
Shortcrust pastry (basic pie crust)	225 g	8 oz	½ lb
Unsalted (sweet) butter	75 g	3 oz	⅓ cup
Caster (superfine) sugar	75 g	3 oz	⅓ cup
Ground almonds	75 g	3 oz	¾ cup
Plain (all-purpose) flour	25 g	1 oz	¼ cup
Egg, beaten	1	1	1
Egg yolk	1	1	1
Ripe pears, peeled and cut into even slices	2	2	2
Apricot jam (conserve)	30 ml	2 tbsp	2 tbsp

1 Line a 25 cm/10 in flan dish (pie pan) with the pastry and leave to chill while preparing the filling.

2 Beat together the butter and sugar until light and fluffy, mix in the ground almonds, flour, beaten egg and egg yolk. Put all of this mixture into the flan dish, level with a spatula and place the pear slices over this, pressing them down slightly.

3 Bake in the oven at 180°C/350°F/gas mark 4 for 45–50 minutes until the flan is golden and firm to the touch.

4 Bring the jam to the boil with 15 ml/1 tbsp water in a small pan, stirring with a wooden spoon. Remove from the heat and sieve (strain) the hot jam, then use this to glaze the flan while it is still warm.

PREPARATION TIME: 15 MINUTES

COOKING TIME: 45–50 MINUTES

Chocolate and Pear Pie

𝒯his pie is best made in advance then heated when ready to eat. The flavour is better when it's just warm.

SERVES 8	METRIC	IMPERIAL	AMERICAN
Flaky pastry (paste)	750 g	1½ lb	1½ lb
Unsalted (sweet) butter	75 g	3 oz	⅓ cup
Caster (superfine) sugar	75 g	3 oz	⅓ cup
Egg	1	1	1
Soured (dairy sour) cream	150 ml	¼ pt	⅔ cup
Self-raising (self-rising) flour	100 g	4 oz	1 cup
Ground ginger	2.5 ml	½ tsp	½ tsp
Cocoa (unsweetened chocolate) powder	15 ml	1 tbsp	1 tbsp
Ground almonds	25 g	1 oz	¼ cup
Can pear halves, drained, reserving juice	425 g	15 oz	1 large
A little milk, egg yolk and caster sugar to glaze			

1 Cut the pastry in half and roll out to form circles, one 20 cm/8 in diameter, the other 23 cm/9 in. Place the small circle on a greased baking sheet.

2 Beat together the butter and sugar until pale and fluffy, then beat in the egg and stir in the cream, flour, ginger, cocoa and almonds.

3 Spread this mixture on to the pastry, leaving a small border all around the edge. Top with the pears. Brush the edge with a little milk or cream. Place the larger pastry circle on top and press the edges together to seal. Knock up with the back of a knife.

4   Decorate the top with a sharp knife. Brush with milk and egg yolk. Sprinkle with sugar and bake in the oven at 200°C/400°F/gas mark 6 for 40–45 minutes.

PREPARATION TIME: 15 MINUTES
COOKING TIME: 40–45 MINUTES

Meringue Fruit Crush

This is a dessert which can be made from bought meringues, frozen fruits plus UHT cream and yet will not taste in the least like a standby recipe, especially if you add a little icing sugar and vanilla essence to the cream when you whip it.

SERVES 6	METRIC	IMPERIAL	AMERICAN
Double (heavy) cream	450 ml	¾ pt	2 cups
Colourful summer fruits	350 g	12 oz	3 cups
Meringues, lightly crushed	175 g	6 oz	1½ cups
Toasted hazelnuts OR almonds	50 g	2 oz	⅓ cup

TO DECORATE
Grated chocolate

1   Whip the cream until it forms soft peaks. Layer the fruits, crushed meringues and nuts in 6 glasses, finishing with a layer of cream.

2   Decorate with grated chocolate and chill to allow the flavours to develop and the meringues to soften slightly before serving.

PREPARATION TIME: 5 MINUTES PLUS CHILLING TIME

Caledonian Mousse

*T*his glorious blend of simple ingredients makes a rich and delicious dessert.

SERVES 6	METRIC	IMPERIAL	AMERICAN
Whisky	30 ml	2 tbsp	2 tbsp
Ginger marmalade	30 ml	2 tbsp	2 tbsp
Finely grated rind of ½ lemon			
Lemon juice	15 ml	1 tbsp	1 tbsp
Caster (superfine) sugar	30 ml	2 tbsp	2 tbsp
Double (heavy) cream	300 ml	½ pt	1¼ cups
Egg whites	2	2	2

TO SERVE
Brandy snaps

1   Put the whisky, marmalade, lemon rind, juice and sugar into a bowl and leave for 15 minutes.

2   Stir the cream into this mixture until blended and then beat till thick.

3   Whisk the egg whites until stiff, fold into the whipped cream mixture and spoon into individual dishes. Chill for 30 minutes before serving with brandy snaps.

PREPARATION TIME: 20 MINUTES PLUS CHILLING TIME

Meringue Peaches

These peaches look very pretty and are a nice light and fruity end to any meal. Try using small squares of chocolate or ginger cake instead of amaretti biscuits.

SERVES 4	METRIC	IMPERIAL	AMERICAN
Canned peach halves	4	4	4
Amaretti biscuits	4	4	4
Orange liqueur	30 ml	2 tbsp	2 tbsp
Egg white	1	1	1
Caster (superfine) sugar	50 g	2 oz	¼ cup
Flaked almonds	25 g	1 oz	¼ cup
Icing (confectioner's) sugar, for dusting			

1   Dry the peaches on kitchen paper and place hollow side up on a greased baking sheet.

2   Put an amaretti biscuit inside each one. Drizzle the liqueur over.

3   Whisk the egg white until stiff then gradually whisk in the sugar.

4   Using a teaspoon, top the peaches with the meringue and sprinkle with the almonds.

5   Bake in the oven at 200°C/400°F/gas mark 6 until the meringue is a pale golden brown. Lightly dust with icing sugar and serve at once.

PREPARATION TIME: 8 MINUTES	
COOKING TIME: 5–10 MINUTES	

Brandy Snap Baskets

*T*his is a basic brandy snap recipe, but instead of rolling the snaps around the spoon handle, you mould them around a small dish, jar or an orange. This recipe makes more than 8, but I have allowed for breakages, and cook's samples! When the baskets are completely cold, you can line them with melted chocolate; this clogs up the lacy holes and allows you to fill them with more moist fillings.

SERVES 8	METRIC	IMPERIAL	AMERICAN
Unsalted (sweet) butter	50 g	2 oz	¼ cup
Caster (superfine) sugar	50 g	2 oz	¼ cup
Golden (light corn) syrup	30 ml	2 tbsp	2 tbsp
Plain (all-purpose) flour	50 g	2 oz	½ cup
Ground ginger	2.5 ml	½ tsp	½ tsp
Brandy	5 ml	1 tsp	1 tsp
Finely grated rind of ½ lemon			

FILLING			
Fresh fruits and/or ice cream			

1   Line 2 baking sheets with baking parchment.

2   Melt the butter, sugar and syrup together over a low heat. Remove from the heat.

3   Sift in the flour and ginger together with the brandy and lemon rind. Mix thoroughly with a wooden spoon and leave to cool for 1–2 minutes.

4   Drop the mixture on to the baking sheets using 10 ml/2 tsp at a time and spacing at 10 cm/4 in intervals. Bake in the oven at 180°C/350°F/gas mark 4 for 7–10 minutes or until the snaps are bubbly, golden brown and lacy in texture.

5 Remove from the oven and quickly mould round inverted individual dishes, then cool on a wire rack.

6 Fill with fresh fruit and/or scoops of ice cream just before serving.

PREPARATION TIME: 15 MINUTES

COOKING TIME: 7–10 MINUTES

Strawberry Crunch

*T*his is delicious in its own right, but it also makes the perfect filling for a pavlova. Substitute crushed brandy snaps for amaretti biscuits for a change.

SERVES 6	METRIC	IMPERIAL	AMERICAN
Double (heavy) cream	300 ml	½ pt	1¼ cups
Caster (superfine) sugar	25 g	1 oz	2 tbsp
Strawberries	350 g	12 oz	3 cups
Amaretti biscuits (cookies), roughly crushed	50 g	2 oz	4 tbsp

1 Whip the cream and sugar until stiff.

2 Chop the strawberries, reserving 6 whole ones for decoration.

3 Fold the crushed biscuits and chopped strawberries into the cream. Pile into individual dishes. Decorate with reserved strawberries and serve.

PREPARATION TIME: 5 MINUTES

Frozen Coffee Crunch Soufflés

*T*hese luscious individual soufflés must be made in advance to allow time for freezing. Place them in the fridge to soften slightly while you serve the main course.

SERVES 4	METRIC	IMPERIAL	AMERICAN
Egg whites	2	2	2
Caster (superfine) sugar	175 g	6 oz	¾ cup
Instant coffee	7.5 ml	1½ tsp	1½ tsp
Boiling water	7.5 ml	1½ tsp	1½ tsp
Grand Marnier	15 ml	1 tbsp	1 tbsp
Double (heavy) cream	375 ml	13 fl oz	1½ cups
Amaretti biscuits (cookies), crushed	12	12	12
Icing (confectioner's) sugar, for dusting			
Toasted almonds	4	4	4

1   Line 4 ramekins (custard cups) with greaseproof (waxed) paper collars to stand 5 cm/2 in above the rims. Whisk the egg whites until stiff.

2   Dissolve the sugar in 90 ml/6 tbsp of water, then boil for 3 minutes without stirring. Pour this caramel on to the egg whites in a thin stream, whisking at high speed until cool.

3   Dissolve the coffee in the boiling water and stir in the liqueur. Whisk into the meringue.

4   Whip the cream until softly peaking and fold into the egg mixture. Half-fill the ramekins and sprinkle with a thick layer of crushed amaretti biscuits. Top with the soufflé mixture to 2.5 cm/1 in above the rims. Freeze for at least 2 hours, then remove the collars and coat the raised edges with the remaining biscuits, dust with icing sugar and top with a toasted almond before serving.

PREPARATION TIME: 20 MINUTES PLUS FREEZING TIME

Caramelised Pear Pizza

*T*his is the sort of dessert you don't need to be hungry to eat even though it's quite rich.

SERVES 6	METRIC	IMPERIAL	AMERICAN
Flaky pastry (paste)	225 g	8 oz	½ lb
Butter, softened	15 g	½ oz	1 tbsp
Caster (superfine) sugar	200 g	7 oz	scant 1 cup
Ripe pears, peeled, cored and sliced	3	3	3
Mascarpone cheese	30 ml	2 tbsp	2 tbsp

TO SERVE
Single (light) cream OR vanilla ice cream

1 Roll out the pastry to form a 25 cm/10 in circle, place on a dampened baking sheet and bake in the oven at 190°C/375°F/gas mark 5 for about 6 minutes. Remove from the oven and set aside while making the topping.

2 Melt the butter in a frying pan (skillet) and add the sugar, stirring. When this mixture starts to turn golden, add the pear slices and keep tossing them over a high heat until they are caramelised. Add a little water if they start to stick (be careful of any spluttering).

3 Arrange the pears over the pastry and dot with the mascarpone cheese. Bake in the oven at the same temperature as before for about 15 minutes until the pastry is well risen and the pears are golden brown. Serve warm with a jug of cream or vanilla ice cream.

PREPARATION TIME: 20 MINUTES
COOKING TIME: 21 MINUTES

Tiramisu

I think it's best to make Tiramisu the day before you need it, as this gives the flavours time to develop.

SERVES 6	METRIC	IMPERIAL	AMERICAN
Mascarpone cheese	250 g	9 oz	good 1 cup
Eggs, separated	4	4	4
Caster (superfine) sugar	60 ml	4 tbsp	4 tbsp
Strong coffee	10 ml	2 tsp	2 tsp
Plain (semi-sweet) chocolate, cut into small pieces	100 g	4 oz	¼ lb
Weak coffee	120 ml	4 fl oz	½ cup
Amaretto OR coffee liqueur	90 ml	6 tbsp	6 tbsp
Sponge fingers	20	20	20

TO DECORATE
Drinking (sweetened) chocolate powder

1   Whisk the cheese and egg yolks together and gradually add the sugar. Mix in the strong coffee.

2   Whisk the egg whites until stiff and fold into the cheese mixture. Add the chocolate pieces and stir gently.

3   Mix together the weak coffee and liqueur and dip half the fingers in this one at a time and use to line the bottom of a serving dish. Pour in half the cheese mixture and then dip the remaining fingers in the liqueur coffee mixture and lay on top of the cheese.

4   Pour over the remaining cheese mixture, bang the dish down lightly to help settle the layers.

5   Chill until ready to serve. Just before serving dust with drinking chocolate powder.

PREPARATION TIME: 20 MINUTES PLUS CHILLING TIME

Valentine Apples

SERVES 6	METRIC	IMPERIAL	AMERICAN
Flaky pastry (paste)	450 g	1 lb	1 lb
Beaten egg, for glazing			
Icing (confectioner's) sugar, for dusting			
White marzipan	175 g	6 oz	⅓ lb
Crisp green eating (dessert) apples	2	2	2
Butter, melted	25 g	1 oz	2 tbsp
Caster (superfine) sugar	45 ml	3 tbsp	3 tbsp

TO SERVE			
Cream			

1 Make 2 heart-shaped templates, one measuring 10 cm/ 4 in at its widest point and the other 2 cm/1 in smaller all round. Roll out the pastry and, using the larger template, cut out 6 hearts. Place on a dampened baking sheet and brush with beaten egg.

2 Dust the work surface with icing sugar and roll out the marzipan. Using the small template, cut out 6 hearts and place these on top of the pastry hearts. Peel and slice the apples and arrange 3 or 4 slices on each heart in a fan shape. Brush with melted butter and sprinkle over the caster sugar.

3 Bake in the oven at 220°C/425°F/gas mark 7 for 15 minutes until the pastry is golden and the apples are cara- melised. Serve warm with cream.

PREPARATION TIME: 25 MINUTES
COOKING TIME: 15 MINUTES

Brandy Chocolate Roulade

*T*his roulade is best served chilled and can be made in advance, frozen for up to 3 months and then thawed at room temperature before serving.

SERVES 8	METRIC	IMPERIAL	AMERICAN
Oil, for greasing			
Plain (semi-sweet) chocolate	175 g	6 oz	1¼ cups
Hot water	30 ml	2 tbsp	2 tbsp
Eggs (size 1), separated	5	5	5
Caster (superfine) sugar	175 g	6 oz	¾ cup
FILLING			
Double (heavy) cream	150 ml	¼ pt	⅔ cup
Soured (dairy sour) cream	150 ml	¼ pt	⅔ cup
Brandy	30 ml	2 tbsp	2 tbsp
Caster (superfine) sugar, for dusting			
TO DECORATE			
Chocolate curls			

1   Line a 23 × 33 cm/9 × 13 in Swiss roll tin (jelly roll pan) with greaseproof (waxed) paper, cut large enough to extend slightly above the sides. Oil lightly.

2   Melt the chocolate and stir in the hot water and sugar. Whisk in the egg yolks.

3   Whisk the egg whites until stiff and fold into the chocolate mix. Pour into the prepared tin. Bake in the oven at 200°C/400°F/gas mark 6 for 15 minutes. Leave to cool for 2 hours.

4   Make the filling. Whip the double cream until softly peaking, then fold in the soured cream and brandy.

5   When the roulade is cold, invert it on to some greaseproof paper, dusted with caster sugar. Remove the lining paper and trim the edges. Spread the filling over, roll up and decorate with chocolate curls.

PREPARATION TIME: 15 MINUTES PLUS CHILLING

COOKING TIME: 15 MINUTES

Cookie Log

The original of this dessert was made with gingernuts and sherry and this, of course, makes an excellent alternative.

SERVES 4	METRIC	IMPERIAL	AMERICAN
Chocolate cookies	200 g	7 oz	7 oz
Port	45 ml	3 tbsp	3 tbsp
Brandy	45 ml	3 tbsp	3 tbsp
Whipped cream	450 ml	¾ pt	2 cups

TO DECORATE
Grated chocolate OR toasted flaked almonds

1   Dip the biscuits in the port and brandy and sandwich together with three quarters of the cream.

2   Use the rest of the cream to cover the biscuit log. Decorate with the chocolate or almonds.

3   Chill for at least 3 hours before serving so that the cookies start to soften and the cream begins to absorb the boozy chocolate flavour.

PREPARATION TIME: 10 MINUTES PLUS CHILLING TIME

Whisky Oranges with Atholl Brose Cream

*T*his dessert can be made a couple of days in advance so that the flavours really mingle with each other.

SERVES 8	METRIC	IMPERIAL	AMERICAN
Granulated sugar	200 g	7 oz	scant 1 cup
Water	150 ml	¼ pt	⅔ cup
Whisky	75 ml	5 tbsp	⅓ cup
Oranges	8	8	8
Double (heavy) cream	450 ml	¾ pt	2 cups
Clear honey	45 ml	3 tbsp	3 tbsp
Whisky	45 ml	3 tbsp	3 tbsp

1 Stir the granulated sugar and water over a low heat until the sugar dissolves. Bring to the boil and simmer for 2 minutes. Remove from the heat, add the whisky and leave to cool.

2 Remove all the rind and pith from the oranges and cut into segments, cutting between the membranes. Put these segments into a bowl and pour the syrup over.

3 To make the Atholl Brose cream, whip the cream until it is softly peaking. Put the honey and whisky into a bowl and stir until well blended. Gradually whisk into the cream until thick. Chill until ready to serve. Spoon the oranges and syrup into 8 bowls and top with the Atholl Brose cream.

PREPARATION TIME: 25 MINUTES PLUS CHILLING TIME

Scarlet Salad

This is really a summertime dessert because it tastes best when made with firm fresh fruits.

SERVES 6	METRIC	IMPERIAL	AMERICAN
Redcurrants	225 g	8 oz	2 cups
Raspberries	225 g	8 oz	2 cups
Small sweet strawberries	225 g	8 oz	2 cups
Sugar	60 ml	4 tbsp	4 tbsp
Lemon juice	15 ml	1 tbsp	1 tbsp
Orange juice	30 ml	2 tbsp	2 tbsp
Amaretti biscuits (cookies), crushed	6	6	6

1   Layer the fruits and sugar in a large bowl. Add the lemon juice and orange juice, cover and chill for several hours.

2   Pile fruit and their scarlet juices into glasses for serving and top with crushed amaretti biscuits – no cream is needed.

PREPARATION TIME: 5 MINUTES PLUS CHILLING TIME

Chocolate Mallow Pie

*A*ll true pudding lovers will swoon with delight when they taste this.

SERVES 6	METRIC	IMPERIAL	AMERICAN
Chocolate digestive biscuits (graham crackers), crushed	200 g	7 oz	1¾ cups
Butter, melted	75 g	3 oz	⅓ cup
Plain (semi-sweet) chocolate	100 g	4 oz	1 cup
Marshmallows (pink and white type)	20	20	20
Water	30 ml	2 tbsp	2 tbsp
Egg, separated	1	1	1
Double (heavy) cream, whipped	300 ml	½ pt	1¼ cups
TO DECORATE			
Extra whipped cream			

1 Mix the biscuits and butter together and use to line an 18 cm/7 in flan dish (pie pan).

2 Melt the chocolate with the marshmallows and water, cool slightly, then stir in the egg yolk and leave to cool.

3 Whisk the egg white until stiff and fold into the chocolate mixture with the whipped cream. Pour on to the biscuit base and chill until set. Decorate with the extra cream before serving.

PREPARATION TIME: 15 MINUTES PLUS COOLING AND CHILLING TIME

Norwegian Cream

*T*here are many recipes called 'Norwegian Cream', but this is much simpler than most. Use orange liqueur instead of juice if you prefer.

SERVES 9	METRIC	IMPERIAL	AMERICAN
Eggs, separated	9	9	9
Caster (superfine) sugar	175 g	6 oz	¾ cup
Gelatine	20 g	¾ oz	1½ tbsp
Orange juice	30 ml	2 tbsp	2 tbsp
FOR TOPPING			
Jam (conserve)			
Whipped cream			
TO DECORATE			
Grated chocolate			

1 Whisk the whites until stiff. Add the sugar and whisk again until peaking.

2 Whisk the yolks, fold in the whites.

3 Dissolve the gelatine in the orange juice in a bowl over a pan of hot water (or in the microwave). Fold into the eggs. Pour into a big shallow dish. Chill until set.

4 When set, spread jam on top. Spread the whipped cream over. Decorate with grated chocolate.

PREPARATION TIME: 10 MINUTES PLUS CHILLING TIME

Apple and Orange Brûlée

*Y*ou can use a mixture of double cream and yoghurt instead of crème fraîche if you prefer.

SERVES 4	METRIC	IMPERIAL	AMERICAN
Crème fraîche	175 ml	6 fl oz	¾ cup
Small apples, cored and diced	2	2	2
Small oranges, peeled and chopped	2	2	2
Soft brown OR granulated sugar	100 g	4 oz	½ cup

1 Mix all the ingredients except the sugar together and place in a shallow heatproof dish. Chill well.

2 Spread brown sugar on top of the fruit mixture and put under a hot grill (broiler) for about 2 minutes until the sugar caramelises. Chill until needed. Alternatively, add a drop of water to the granulated sugar and put in the microwave in a heatproof dish and cook on high until it forms a light yellow toffee. Pour over the fruit mixture and chill until needed.

3 To serve: bring to the table straight from the fridge and bang the toffee with a metal spoon. This cracks the top and makes it easy to serve.

PREPARATION AND COOKING TIME: 5 MINUTES PLUS
CHILLING TIME

Oranges with Yoghurt Sauce

*T*his is a very light summery pudding which is ideal after a rich main course.

SERVES 4	METRIC	IMPERIAL	AMERICAN
Oranges, peeled	4	4	4
Salt and freshly ground black OR white pepper			
Roasted cumin seeds, ground			
Cayenne			
Plain yoghurt	250 ml	8 fl oz	1 cup
Fresh root ginger, finely grated	5 ml	1 tsp	1 tsp
Sugar	20 ml	4 tsp	4 tsp

1   Cut the oranges into 5–6 slices and then cut each slice in half again crosswise.

2   Sprinkle one side very lightly with salt, pepper, cumin and cayenne. On 4 serving plates arrange slices in a slightly overlapping circle, leaving a gap in the middle. Cover and chill.

3   Blend the yoghurt with the ginger, sugar and a pinch of salt, pepper, cumin and cayenne until smooth and creamy. Just before serving, put a dollop of this mixture in the centre of the orange slices.

PREPARATION TIME: 10 MINUTES

Lemon Curd Mousse

*T*his is even better if you serve it sprinkled with grated plain (semi-sweet) chocolate.

SERVES 6	METRIC	IMPERIAL	AMERICAN
Gelatine	7.5 ml	1½ tsp	1½ tsp
Eggs, separated	3	3	3
Caster (superfine) sugar	100 g	4 oz	½ cup
Grated rind and juice of 2 small lemons			
Butter	65 g	2½ oz	good ¼ cup

1   Sprinkle the gelatine on to 30 ml/2 tbsp of water and leave to soften.

2   Whisk the egg yolks and all but 25 g/1 oz/2 tbsp of the sugar, until thick and pale.

3   Put the lemon rind, lemon juice and butter in a saucepan and bring to the boil. Add the soaked gelatine and put into a food processor or blender and run the machine for 1½–2 minutes with the yolk mixture.

4   Whisk whites until just peaking. Whisk in the remaining sugar and fold in the hot lemon mixture. Turn into individual glass serving dishes and chill for 4–6 hours before serving.

PREPARATION TIME: 10 MINUTES PLUS CHILLING TIME

Chocolate Mousse

This is a fool-proof method as long as you have a food processor.

SERVES 6	METRIC	IMPERIAL	AMERICAN
Eggs, separated	4	4	4
Plain (semi-sweet) chocolate	200 g	7 oz	1¾ cups
Strong hot coffee	75 ml	5 tbsp	5 tbsp
Vanilla essence (extract)	2.5 ml	½ tsp	½ tsp

TO DECORATE
A little whipped cream and drinking (sweetened) chocolate powder

1　Whisk the egg whites until stiff.

2　Break up the chocolate and put into a food processor or blender. Run the machine until the chocolate is completely crushed.

3　Add the hot coffee and blend until smooth. Add the yolks and vanilla essence and blend for about 1 minute.

4　Pour the chocolate mixture slowly over the egg whites and fold in lightly but thoroughly.

5　Spoon into individual dishes or a large serving dish and chill for about 1 hour.

6　Top with whipped cream and a sprinkling of drinking chocolate powder.

PREPARATION TIME: 10 MINUTES PLUS CHILLING TIME

Crêpes with Chocolate Cream

*T*he chocolate mousse-type mixture is good enough to eat as a chocolate mousse in its own right, but is also wonderful as a filling for ready-made crêpes.

SERVES 4	METRIC	IMPERIAL	AMERICAN
Strawberries	4	4	4
Kirsch	30 ml	2 tbsp	2 tbsp
Whipping cream	150 ml	¼ pt	⅓ cup
Drinking (sweetened) chocolate powder	30 ml	2 tbsp	2 tbsp
Grated chocolate	30 ml	2 tbsp	2 tbsp
Crêpes	4	4	4
Icing (confectioner's) sugar, for dusting			

1   Wash the strawberries but do not hull. Cut diagonally through the strawberries just to the calyx so they fan out. Soak in kirsch until needed.

2   Whisk the cream with the drinking chocolate powder and grated chocolate.

3   Open out the crêpes and spread with chcolate mixture, roll up and top each with a strawberry. Dust with icing sugar and serve.

PREPARATION TIME: 5 MINUTES

Kiwi Pavlova

*E*veryone says they either can or can't make pavlovas – yet they are so simple, I can't see where the mystique comes from!

SERVES 8	METRIC	IMPERIAL	AMERICAN
Egg whites	4	4	4
Caster (superfine) sugar	225 g	8 oz	1 cup
Cornflour (cornstarch)	15 ml	1 tbsp	1 tbsp
Vanilla essence (extract)	1.5 ml	¼ tsp	¼ tsp
Vinegar	10 ml	2 tsp	2 tsp
FILLING			
Whipped cream			
Kiwifruit, sliced			

1 Whisk the egg whites until stiff, and add the sugar gradually.

2 Add the remaining ingredients.

3 Spoon on to a greased baking sheet or (preferably) baking parchment on the sheet. Bake at 150°C/300°F/gas mark 2 for 1½ hours. When cool, fill the centre with whipped cream and sliced kiwifruit.

PREPARATION TIME: 10 MINUTES
COOKING TIME: 1½ HOURS

Banoffee Pie

SERVES 6	METRIC	IMPERIAL	AMERICAN
BASE			
Biscuits (cookies), crushed	200 g	7 oz	1¾ cups
Butter, melted	50 g	2 oz	¼ cup
FILLING			
Can sweetened condensed milk	350 g	12 oz	1 large
Bananas, sliced	3	3	3
Double (heavy) cream	300 ml	½ pt	1¼ cups
Caster (superfine) sugar	30 ml	2 tbsp	2 tbsp
Instant coffee	15 ml	1 tbsp	1 tbsp
TO DECORATE			
Drinking (sweetened) chocolate powder OR grated chocolate			

1   Put the unopened can of milk in a saucepan of boiling water. Simmer for at least 3 hours, keeping the tin submerged all the time. Allow to cool in the water (I boil a few at a time and have them in the pantry ready to use).

2   Make the base by mixing the crumbs with the melted butter. Press into a flan dish (pie pan). Chill until firm.

3   Spread the cold caramelised milk on to the base. Top with sliced bananas.

4   Whip the cream, sugar and coffee powder together and pipe on to the bananas. Decorate with chocolate powder or grated chocolate. Chill until ready to serve.

PREPARATION TIME: 15 MINUTES PLUS BOILING TIME FOR
THE CAN OF MILK AND CHILLING TIME

Tom's Chocolate Gateau

*T*his is a really moist mix, so care has to be taken when slicing it in two before filling.

SERVES 6	METRIC	IMPERIAL	AMERICAN
Plain (all-purpose) flour	175 g	6 oz	1½ cups
Granulated sugar	175 g	6 oz	¾ cup
Cocoa (unsweetened) chocolate powder	50 g	2 oz	½ cup
Salt	2.5 ml	½ tsp	½ tsp
Bicarbonate of soda (baking soda)	5 ml	1 tsp	1 tsp
Vanilla essence (extract)	5 ml	1 tsp	1 tsp
Cider vinegar	15 ml	1 tbsp	1 tbsp
Sunflower oil	120 ml	4 fl oz	½ cup
Water	250 ml	8 fl oz	1 cup

TO FILL AND TOP
Black cherry jam (conserve), whipped cream and a little grated chocolate

1 Grease and line a 20 cm/8 in cake tin.

2 Combine the flour, sugar, cocoa, salt and bicarbonate of soda. Make a well in the centre and add the vanilla, vinegar, oil and water. Mix until just blended.

3 Turn into the prepared tin. Bake at 190°C/375°F/gas mark 5 for 40 minutes. Leave to cool in the tin on a wire rack for 10 minutes, then turn out and leave to cool.

4 When cold, split in two and fill with jam and whipped cream. Spread cream on the top and sprinkle with chocolate.

PREPARATION TIME: 10 MINUTES

COOKING TIME: 40 MINUTES PLUS COOLING TIME

Crème Caramel

*E*ven after a large dinner one of these always slips down easily – it is the perfect 'second pud'.

SERVES 6	METRIC	IMPERIAL	AMERICAN
CARAMEL			
Caster (superfine) sugar	175 g	6 oz	¾ cup
Cold water	60 ml	4 tbsp	4 tbsp
CUSTARD			
Single (light) cream	750 ml	1¼ pts	3 cups
Egg yolks	6	6	6
Caster (superfine) sugar	15 ml	1 tbsp	1 tbsp
Vanilla essence (extract)	5 ml	1 tsp	1 tsp

1   Put the caster sugar, for the caramel, in a pan with the cold water. Heat gently until the syrup is clear, then boil without stirring until it turns a golden caramel colour. Pour into 6 ramekins (custard cups) and leave to cool.

2   Put the cream, egg yolks beaten with the sugar and vanilla essence into a bowl over a pan of simmering water. Cook gently until the cream thickens whisking gently. Pour through a sieve (strainer) into the ramekins. Chill until cold and set.

3   You can either turn them out or eat as they are.

PREPARATION TIME: 30 MINUTES PLUS CHILLING TIME

Bananas with Brandy Caramel Sauce

*T*his is a delicious, rich dessert prepared in minutes. The sauce is also great with ice cream.

SERVES 6	METRIC	IMPERIAL	AMERICAN
Piece of cinnamon stick	5 cm	2 in	2 in
Juice of 1 orange			
Brown sugar	15 ml	1 tbsp	1 tbsp
Bananas	6	6	6
Cointreau	30 ml	2 tbsp	2 tbsp
SAUCE			
Mars Bars	4	4	4
Water	30 ml	2 tbsp	2 tbsp
Brandy	30 ml	2 tbsp	2 tbsp

1 Prepare the bananas first as the sauce has to be made just before serving. Put the cinnamon, orange juice and sugar in a pan over a low heat so the sugar dissolves.

2 Thickly slice the bananas diagonally and add to the pan. Cook for 5 minutes, adding the Cointreau half-way through cooking.

3 Chop the Mars Bars finely, put into another pan and melt on very low heat, adding enough water to keep runny. Add the brandy, stir until blended and serve over the bananas.

PREPARATION TIME: 5 MINUTES
COOKING TIME: 5 MINUTES

Index